WHAT OTHERS

'This is the very personal story gave themselves to serve the Lord in the nation of Spain. They could have chosen very different career paths, having had the education and training to do so. This is their story, the highs and the lows, lessons learnt some the hard way but also of divine connections and appointments. Read and be inspired, challenged and learn from them the modern missionary calling of what it means to walk by faith, plant church and see the kingdom come.'

Norman Barnes (Founder of Links International)

'This is an inspiring book illustrating the wonder of lives submitted to the King of Kings. It is a story not only of adventure but of transformation of Caroline's own life and of all involved in the journey. She herself says "God changed my fears to faith" and I am sure this should be the goal for all of us. Lives laid down for God and submitted to His calling grow richer in every way and Caroline shows this vividly in the story of their experiences in Spain. The reader will finish catching something of their love for this colourful country – the land of the matador.'

Sue Trudinger (Basingstoke Community Church)

'Caroline's very honest, matter of fact and revealing insights into following the call of God to build His Kingdom, from the initial seed to its fulfilment are both breathtakingly refreshing and challenging. Her very practical approach provides the reader with an insight to her early formative years and the practical outcomes of following God and reveals her tenacious determination.'

Rev. Mervyn G. Ewing (Superintendent Minister of the Lisburn and Dromore Methodist circuit in the Methodist Church in Ireland)

'Caroline's story is one of courage, adventure and a faith in God. It is a delight to read her thoughts and recollections first hand, capturing her love of Spain, her love of people and her love of God.'

Becca Jupp (Senior leader of Arun Community Church, Littlehampton)

'This is the very personal account of Caroline and Desmond Bellew's faith and courage as evangelists and church planters in present day Spain. It will be an inspiration to all who sense the call of God to tell others the good news of Jesus. It is also a reminder, that whatever the challenges faced, the Lord provides for those who serve in His Name.'

Rev. John Dinnen (Former Dean of the Diocese of Down, Northern Ireland)

'How can God work as a master goldsmith to develop in one couple a joint cross-cultural and pioneering call? How can the Lord of the Harvest reveal such a complete and effective world view based on the whole gospel? Caroline and Desmond understood that church-planting is the surest way to preserve and develop, through discipleship, the fruits of evangelism.

As well as recommending with enthusiasm this book to any Christian or more specifically to those who have missionary dreams in their hearts, allow me to honour these missionaries from Northern Ireland. I honour them for their deep love for Spanish and Latin American people, for giving themselves firstly to God and then to their neighbour. This magnificent and sincere story has been ably written by Caroline and is a powerful testimony.'

Ernesto Riquelme Lazo (Co-ordinator of the Mediterranean Project, YWAM Chile)

'When I first met Caroline and Desmond Bellew soon after their arrival in Spain, I sensed that they were people who could impact their city and beyond. As I interacted with them through the years, my first impression was confirmed time and time again. They have left a deep impression on an entire region of Spain. As I read the manuscript, I was delighted in seeing this x-ray of their battles and victories. This book should serve as an inspiration for others who are sensing a call from God to a difficult mission field, as well as believers everywhere!'

Gary McKinney (YWAM leader in Spain since 1974)

Published 2018

Arun Christian Publishing
89 Worthing Road
Rustington BN16 3NA

ISBN: 978-1-9996426-0-0

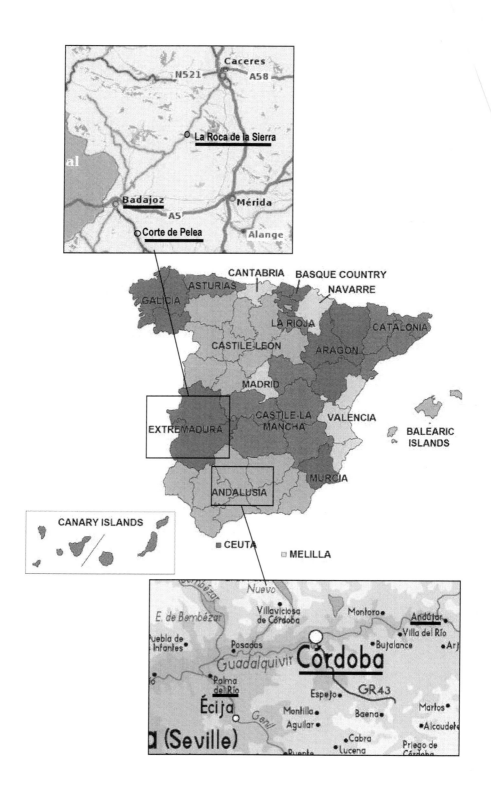

DEDICATION

I dedicate this book to my three wonderful grandchildren, Harry, Sophie and Robbie. I am grateful to them for all the good times we have had together. May they also find their destiny.

CONTENTS

ACKNOWLEDGMENTS

I wish to thank the many friends, both old and new, that have helped me with this book. They are too many to name here. Firstly I must thank my editor Rev Dr. Eric Rogers, Grace Upcraft, my copy editor and proof reader Gweno Hugh-Jones. Then Cleland Thom, owner of College of Media and Publishing and Jennie Harborth, my cover designer. A big thank you to those who kindly took the time out of busy lives to read and recommend my manuscript - Gary McKinney and Nino Riquelme from Spain, Rev. Mervyn Ewing and Rev. John Dinnen from Northern Ireland and Norman Barnes, Becca Jupp and Sue Trudinger from England. Thanks to Sue Chitty for all her encouragement when I most needed it. Last but not least to my husband for his good advice, patience and very necessary help as always on the computer.

PREFACE

When you think of Spain, what springs to mind? Do you think of beautiful sun-scorched beaches, dark-skinned ladies in colourful dresses dancing to flamenco music, fierce bull-fights involving matadors in elaborate costumes? Or do you think of the real Spain, the heart of Spain, where there are very few tourists? What is it really like to live there and meet the people? If this is of interest to you, then this book is for you. Many enjoyable books have been written and enjoyed by myself such as *Driving over lemons* by Chris Stewart. This one is however different and more about the spiritual climate of the country.

Imagine a narrow street in Córdoba, Southern Spain called Santa María de Gracia with the thirteenth century church San Lorenzo at one end. A blaze of colour shone out from the many geranium boxes hanging from the balconies of the houses. The windows had to be open in summer to let in some cooler air after the stifling heat of the day. The street was so narrow that we could hear and easily identify the TV programme watched by our neighbours across the road. That, added to the noise from the bar nearby, meant there was little silence in that environment in the flat which was our home for six years. Of course noise is what we associate with Spain. At night there was silence for a few hours, at least after the bars had closed down. The predominant smells in that area of the town were of garlic and spirits and even the sewers at times, and these wonderful scents were strong enough to remain enveloped in the night air. It was on one of those summer nights that a slightly scary event occurred.

A knock on our bedroom door came in the early hours of the morning. It was Juan Carlos.

'Pepe has a knife and he is threatening to kill us' he gasped as he wiped the sweat from off his brow.

'Don't worry, I'm coming' replied my husband as he got up to see what was happening in the young men's dormitory.

Sure enough, there was Pepe, standing on a bed, brandishing a large kitchen knife...

However did I get myself into this desperate situation in Spain? I suggest you read on if you want to discover the answer to this question.

1 IN THE LAND OF THE MATADOR

A FLASHBACK TO OUR FIRST CHURCH IN SPAIN. A dark shadow flitted through the silent streets of the old Córdoba, sinister in the early hours of the morning. Nobody was about. He reached his destination. Why was he there? What was he after? Even more problematic, how would he get in?

Laboriously he scaled the metal bars of the entrance gate, swung unto the first floor balcony and climbed over the railing. In a half drunken state he stumbled through the open window. With a loud crash he managed to get into our lounge, situated at the front of the house on the first floor. Frightened screams arose from the innocent Danish girls, part of a visiting team from Youth with a Mission (YWAM) as he lumbered through their improvised bedroom.

'Help, help!' or something equivalent in Danish were the startled cries we could hear in our bedroom.

No, it wasn't a burglar. It was Juan Antonio, a young man with a problem with alcohol we were trying to help. He had gone on a binge and just wanted to get to the boys' quarters at the back of the house. By the time my husband and I got there, the culprit had of course disappeared sheepishly into his own bedroom across the corridor.

....

But there was more drama to come. We woke that first morning in Palma del Río, a small town on the border of the provinces of Córdoba and Sevilla. We were lying on foam mattresses on a stone floor. The morning sun peeped through the gaps between the roof tiles and a gentle breeze blew through the glass-less windows. The house was a virtual ruin, a wonderful adventure playground for our six year old son! What were we doing here in this place, with no electricity in the middle of a blazing Spanish summer?

....

1

'Don't have this young man to stay in your home' was the advice given by some missionary friends. 'He's a Colombian. You can't tell what he might be into. You can't trust him. You don't know what he could do. This is very dangerous.'

This sombre advice seemed to be borne out when two plain-clothed policemen arrived at our door. *Were they the dreaded secret police? Had we done something wrong? Were they going to order us out of the country?* Fortunately not; they were asking after someone called Oscar. Trembling in my shoes I replied:

'No, I don't know anyone called Oscar. There is no one of that name staying here.'

Just then my husband arrived to sort the matter out. The young Colombian we knew as Ramiro was actually Oscar Ramiro. It took some hours before my nerves settled again.

You can imagine me thinking more than once: *Help! What have I got myself into?* How exactly did I get myself into these and other equally hairy situations in the land of the matador? This is the story of someone who moved there and the exciting journey fulfilling God's call on her life. Church planters are just ordinary people with strengths and weaknesses. This will become obvious as you read this book.

2 ON YOUR MARK, GET SET, GO!

I was born towards the end of the Second World War. My childhood was spent in quite an idyllic setting in Northern Ireland. The large thatched seventeenth century farmhouse where I was brought up was near a small village named Upper Ballinderry in Co. Antrim.

In 1976 a journalist wrote about the house, which is now a listed building; as 'standing sturdily and has a feeling of ageless tranquillity about it'. In fact in September 2011 my brother John, who still owns the property and lives there with his wife, had the honour of a visit from Prince Charles. The Prince admired both the home and the organic poultry set-up looked after by my brother and capable nephew Jonathan.

My parents were good honest 'salt of the earth' folk who loved us deeply, brought us up well and nothing was spared. I will always be grateful to my parents for the comfortable upbringing and the many good Christian values instilled in us.

FEARS AND INSECURITIES. However, despite this idyllic childhood, I was extremely timid and fearful from an early age. I clearly remember at age seven, with my mother's help, asking God to forgive my sins and asking Him into my life. Of course I realise now that fear is the opposite of faith. Even though I believe I became a Christian at that point, I, because of fear, had to repeat the process several times before being sure I really was a Christian. A relative referred to me as 'Caroline, the little China doll'. In other words as my mother often insinuated to me, I was rather fragile both physically and emotionally.

My fears and anxieties grew over the years and indeed looking back, one would never have guessed that I would find my destiny in the land of the matador. This would involve many adventures that you will later read about.

There was no alcohol in our home except for a little bottle of brandy which my mother surreptitiously brought in to pour over our Christmas cake and pudding. I developed a real fear of anyone who had drunk too much, which probably stems from an incident near Dundrod (some of you may know the famous motor cycle racecourse there). It was an extremely wet and windy night in the middle of winter.

My father was driving us all as a family and suddenly had to swerve the car to avoid a horribly drunk man who walked straight in front of us and was actually slumped over the bonnet of the car when the car abruptly came to a halt. Although my father was obviously somewhat shaken, he tried to assure us saying

'It's ok, it's ok'.

The resultant shock, the screeching of brakes, then the unintelligible conversation with an inebriate man who had one trouser leg completely torn off, are things that remained in my memory for years. I am glad to be able to say, through prayer and various happenings later told in chapter nine, I was freed from the fears resulting from that memory. Who would have imagined I would later be involved in ministry to drug addicts and alcoholics in Spain?

3 GEARING UP FOR MISSION

EARLY INFLUENCES One memory I have from childhood days was the gift of hospitality that my mother seemed to have. She loved to invite family and friends for beautiful meals at our large dining room table. The most special guests were missionaries from the many foreign missions that my parents supported. There was one lady who spent time in Israel from time to time evangelising among the Jews and her work was very secretive though I was never told why. I had to accept that it was something I would understand when I grew up, which is never a satisfactory answer for a child. As they told their stories over the meal table I began to admire these very different people. So it is not at all surprising that I started to think about being a missionary myself one day.

One occasion stands out when some missionaries came from South America to speak in our local Parish Church (Church of Ireland). They were from the South American Missionary Society (SAMS as it was then known). Their slides and their stories made a big impression on me as a 9 year old. From then on I had a real desire to visit South America and do what I could to relieve the poverty there with the power of the Gospel. You will read in chapter 23 how God later fulfilled that desire of my heart and allowed me to travel to several South American countries. We also received many of their people in our churches in Spain.

LOVE FOR FOREIGN LANGUAGES. At my Quaker school I soon gained a love and certain ability for foreign languages; studying French, German and Spanish up to A-Level. In 1962 those three languages were taken in my first year at Queen's University, Belfast. However in those days one could only study two foreign languages at degree level so I had to choose. My natural choice was to drop Spanish and continue only with French and German. This choice was based on visits to each of these three European countries and Spain simply did not appeal to me.

The family I had stayed with in Barcelona was a very poor Christian family and some of the hygiene in the home had rather turned my stomach. We were given the same supper (Spanish omelette with salad) each evening for a month, which didn't exactly attract me to Spanish cooking. My friend and I were followed on several occasions when coming home from classes at the university. Fortunately a lady who lived above had noticed this man peer in through a slit in our bedroom window as we were undressing. She got an enormous bowl of water one evening and poured it over him. Needless to say he fled and we were no longer bothered by him.

On another occasion two Spanish students tried to deceive us and pull us into a brothel.

'Run for it' I shouted and we escaped just in time.

Moreover I struggled with the spontaneity of the Spaniards and the lack of order at times was so against my somewhat perfectionist tendencies. I later learnt to love that spontaneity.

In the summer of 1963 I was enjoying a five-week stay in Klostermühle, the German Christian centre for the 'Torchbearers' association. Its headquarters was based then at Capernwray Hall, UK. As I attended the conferences and Bible Studies there especially geared for youth, I began to feel uneasy about continuing my German studies. There was no logical reason for this at the time. Back in Belfast I was asked to interpret for a Spanish couple who arrived at a street meeting being held by our university Christian Union. I played an active role in this as publicity secretary and then treasurer. The couple had been walking past. Since they were from the Franco era in Spain where such happenings were completely forbidden, they were obviously curious.

'What is happening here?' they asked.

I can remember the tears in their eyes as I, in my faltering Spanish shared the gospel message with them. The whole experience gave me such tremendous joy and I began to wonder if I wasn't going to do this more often in Spain itself. The final blow to my desire to continue with German was when my university tutor gently told me

'It is obvious from your first year exam results that you should continue with French and Spanish. Your marks in those two languages are rather higher than your German one'.

A verse from the Bible that has helped me in many moments of important decisions was becoming a reality 'In his heart a man plans his course, but the Lord determines his steps.' Proverbs 16:9. It was the beginning of a journey which would take me to Spain to find my destiny. God was leading each step of the way despite all my doubts and fears and indeed lack of desire to live in that beautiful country.

EXCITING EXPERIENCES IN FRANCE. My year in France was a very significant period of my life and one that changed my destiny. This came after finishing my degree course in 1965. At university I had lived quite a sheltered kind of existence mainly surrounded by Christian friends I had chosen or at least those with reasonable moral standards. However in France I could not easily choose my friends. I was thrown together with a group of English, German and Spanish students. We were all teaching assistants in local schools in a small town in Southern France called Agen (famous for its prunes).

Most of them loved to drink a lot and I was a teetotaller as my parents had taught me. My fears of drunken men were still very deep inside me which didn't help when I went to their parties. They needed to hear about God I decided so I invited them to come and meet the pastor of the evangelical church I was attending. He was an academic so I was sure he could answer their questions and many arguments against Christianity. He did his best but my colleagues were not impressed. I decided to try again.

This time I invited them to a small church called the Apostolic church which I also visited from time to time. I discovered that this group of churches had come from the Welsh revival at the beginning of the 20th century. There I saw supernatural healing through the laying on of hands for the first time in my life and it was mainly from an old uneducated French lady. The reaction of my colleagues was so different this time. One commented as he walked out with the others before the end of the meeting,

'Caroline, there is something very real there but I am afraid of getting caught up in it all.'

In other words he noticed the strong presence of the Holy Spirit but did not want to change his way of life.

In those days my experience of God left little space for the Holy Spirit.

'Don't all Christians have the Holy Spirit?' I argued furiously with anyone who tried to suggest I needed another infilling of the same Holy Spirit.

But why then did I find it so hard to live my life as a Christian out in the world among unbelievers? Was that why I was so terrified for days when followed home by Frenchmen late at night and one, living in the same house who even tried to get into my room? For nights I slept with the wardrobe against my door.

By the end of the year I had decided I definitely needed more of God and his Holy Spirit. But it wasn't as simple as that. Another thing I observed for the first time in France was the exercise of spiritual gifts in church services. They assured me it was all biblical and I began to study 1 Corinthians chapters 12, 13 &14. The strangest gift I heard was that of speaking or praying in an unknown tongue. In those days I considered myself somewhat of an expert in languages as one does when at university. I was convinced this gift of tongues was nonsense or at most a psychological phenomenon which could be explained.

Once I went to visit a French friend in another part of France, whom I had met as a helper in a Christian camp the previous year. The camp was for poor and deprived children from Paris. That again was such a new and stressful experience for me that I lost a stone in weight. One of my duties each morning was to search the beds for fleas. I had been brought up well protected and had no idea what a flea looked like. However, this dear French lady had mothered me during that time. I went to her town, only to discover she had to leave me at her church on Sunday morning and go off elsewhere.

To my surprise I found myself in another church that exercised the gifts of the Spirit. I quickly prayed something like this *Lord, this seems no coincidence that I find myself in this sort of church again when I would really rather be in another type of church. It seems as if you want to show me something so Lord I am open.*

An old lady began to sing in tongues and it was in simple Latin which I understood. She was just praising and worshipping God. The interpretation came correctly of course but in my cynicism I thought to myself *that interpreter has probably learnt Latin and is using his mind to interpret the message.* The pastor suddenly announced

'A young English girl is visiting our service today. Please raise your hand if you can take her home for lunch.' I remember noticing a lot of people raising their hands.

The pastor pointed to an elderly couple. They then came forward to meet me and take me home. Strangely enough he had been the man with the interpretation in the service. I felt embarrassed when I arrived at their very isolated simple home in the mountains and saw how poor they seemed to be. However they explained that they had been so lonely last week that they decided to believe that God would send them a visitor for Sunday lunch. In faith they had bought the food in. Over a sumptuous French meal I discovered that this man was completely uneducated and knew no Latin. I felt very humbled and could only conclude that his interpretation had come from the Holy Spirit. Indeed later in life I experienced similar events which have taught me not to doubt the power of the Holy Spirit. But where was all this leading to?

EARLY INFLUENCES. In Northern Ireland it was relatively easy to prepare for mission work abroad. I had learnt all about St. Patrick, the first missionary to Ireland. Statistics of missionaries show the large numbers sent out from that small country. St. Columbanus, educated in Bangor Abbey, Co. Down, was one of the first of many to be sent out to Europe in 590 AD. Before television came to our parts of the country, there was little entertainment for us as teenagers and a very poor bus and train service. Our entertainment was to be taken to a large missionary meeting in either Belfast or Bangor to listen to endless talks from those who had gone to darkest Africa.

Nevertheless one meeting does stand out. We listened spellbound to this small lady called Corrie Ten Boom who gave her amazing story of her time at Ravensbrück as an inmate of one of Hitler's concentration camps. She and her family had rescued and hidden many Jews in their home in Haarlem, Holland. What a living example it was to me then of the importance and possibility of forgiving even our worst enemies! This dear lady once asked

'Is prayer your spare wheel or your steering wheel?'

I would say that from my early twenties it began to be my steering wheel. Prayer became the all important part of my life and in the many decisions that had to be taken.

As well as attending missionary meetings I had read many novels of famous missionaries such as C.T. Studd, Hudson Taylor, David Livingstone, William Carey, Gladys Aylward to name only a few. These were considered the classics. A book about Jim Elliot particularly impacted me. He was the American missionary who was murdered in 1956 along with Nate Saint and three other young men in Ecuador by the indigenous people. His quotations are very famous particularly, 'He is no fool who gives what he cannot keep to gain that which he cannot lose' or 'Wherever you are be all there, live to the hilt every situation you believe to be the will of God.' Little did I know that a group of very similar indigenous Indians from Ecuador would become part of our church in Spain many years later.

Eventually my sister and I persuaded our father to let us have a television at home and for months he said he deeply regretted bringing 'the world' into our sitting room. However it didn't prevent us continuing to read good missionary books. These people I read about were my heroes and became models for later life.

FIRST SUCCESSFUL EVANGELISTIC EFFORT. One big question remained in my mind. If I was called to missions to see people come to know God, did I not need to be able to lead someone to God in my own country first of all? I had never had that thrilling experience but I was preparing to help at a girls' camp for the first time that summer. I was to be in charge of a group of eight teenage girls and when I arrived I discovered that only two of these girls were Christians. In prayer God distinctly told me 'all will be Christians before the end of the camp'. I began to pray for the other six but decided that I would do nothing in my own strength that would persuade these vulnerable lassies to become Christians.

After a few days two of the girls complained of stomach pains and they had to go to bed instead of going to the evening meeting where the gospel was usually well presented. The leader of the camp, an experienced medical consultant, came to see them and found them in tears, very convicted about their sinfulness before God. One by one the same thing happened to the other four. The consultant said that in all her years of Christian girls' camps, she had never seen such a thing. I was finally convinced that the Holy Spirit was at work. All my group were Christians by the end of the two weeks as God had promised. Moreover we kept in touch. About five years later it was so good to meet up with some of those six and discover that all six were continuing in their Christian walk.

PRACTICAL PREPARATION. After my year in France I was offered a month in Bern, Switzerland where I stayed with the family of the pastor I had met in France. This time in their homeland they were speaking German which delighted me. I saw how God is no man's debtor. I had given up studying German in obedience to Him but He, knowing my love for that language and the people who spoke it, was giving me the opportunity to practise it once more. They always had a very open home which I admired and endeavoured to copy later in my own married life. From time to time they took in needy people to live with them in their ample high-rise flat and everyone was made welcome. I had been warned of that beforehand and had agreed that I would help in whatever way I could. These two, Bruno & Elisabet Krähenbuhl, were not much older than myself but they were preparing very seriously to go to plant churches in the Ivory Coast.

FIRST BRUSH WITH PROSTITUTION. A big shock to me when I arrived was to find myself sharing a room with a young Swiss prostitute they were trying to rescue from that lifestyle. The very word prostitute made me shudder! Having been brought up in an era when sex was a rather forbidden word in many households and having seen the misuse of it among many students, I was very innocent. Moreover I was absolutely ignorant of the subject. I really couldn't sleep at first, thinking of what she might want to talk about and thus leaving me clueless. Fortunately she didn't but she was not slow in borrowing my jewellery without even asking. It was not the usual polite British manners I was used to. Several men phoned her and came to collect her.

On one occasion I was outside when the man didn't turn up or perhaps Elisabet had managed to tell him not to come. She lost her temper and began to talk to the other neighbours who were outside the block of flats in the gardens watching their children play. I was horrified to hear her tell the neighbours

'That Elisabet woman is keeping me like a prisoner and I can't escape though I really want to'.

When I repeated what I heard to Elisabet, she simply shrugged her shoulders. What a lesson that was to me who was so concerned about what other people thought of me! Instead Elisabet and her husband were focused on seeing lives lifted out of the mud and won for God.

I had noticed the way they treated this girl as a 'lady', endeavouring always to build up her self-esteem, which is always so low for women in that type of life style. Yes, they did put certain boundaries and limits on her stay but these had been agreed beforehand. Now she was rebelling against those boundaries. I don't remember fifty years later the outcome of that story but I do know it again made a big impression on me. My fear of prostitutes and that unknown world was turning a little to faith in what God can do in changing their lives around. More of this in later chapters.

A TEACHER AT LAST. From an early age I had wanted to be a teacher, so on returning from France I took a year to do the only course then available. This gave me a Diploma in Education allowing me to teach French and Spanish to A-Level with German for beginners. That I proceeded to do in Lisburn, Northern Ireland.

One incident stands out in my memory. I was noticing a lot of rebellion in my third year German class and praying for wisdom. Suddenly one of the girls burst into tears and the class began to tell how some of them had been playing with an ouija board at lunch break. They had been told by the pointer that one of the class, naming her by name, would die very young. I was able to talk to the class about the dangers of this so-called game and even pray aloud there and then for protection and peace for the whole class.

In today's world of course this might not be considered politically correct. The behaviour not only improved but that class surprised all the staff when they presented me later with a very expensive wedding present. I was learning about spiritual warfare which was very necessary for our future work in Spain.

So what was missing from my life?

4 FINDING MR RIGHT

Like most girls in their early twenties, my thoughts turned towards marriage. There were quite a few suitors, including four future ministers, an Anglican, a Presbyterian, a Methodist, and a Seventh Day Adventist! They suddenly appeared on the scene. My favourite verse in those days was, 'Delight yourself in the Lord and He will give you the desire of your heart' Psalm 37:4. I tried to forget about marriage and simply delight myself in Him and let Him bring me the right person. That was during my year in France after my BA degree. I so enjoyed that country that I then began to ask God to give me a French husband but none seemed interested, except very ungodly ones!

Imagine my amazement when just after I came back to Northern Ireland, I met the man who was to become my future husband. One of my first questions was about his unusual surname Bellew. I discovered it was from Normandy in France and came from the words 'Beau lieu' meaning a beautiful place. The Bellews, of whom there were no less than eighteen knights in the direct line of succession, were renowned in the wars of the Middle Ages. I had met my appropriate suitor, a 'fighter' to accompany me to the land of the matador. It was only in later life that I came to realise how helpful his qualities would be for me as we sought to establish churches in Spain.

Here is how our romance developed. Some other students at university had told me about this Desmond Bellew who was very passionate about seeking God in prayer. As well as attending the Christian Union and all his own church activities, he had begun a special prayer meeting. Its aim was to seek the Holy Spirit in the way I had come across in that church in France. Immediately an inner voice seemed to say to me, 'He will be your husband'.

One lunch time I was sitting in the student dining hall with a friend and noticed this young man pass by wearing a Christian badge in his lapel. His face was glowing and I began to wonder if that could be him, my future husband. My friend knew the story.

She dared me to go up and ask him his name. This I did rather nervously and when I realised my intuition had been correct I was quite speechless. I began to attend his prayer meetings and finally had a dramatic experience as in Acts 10:44-48. I spoke in tongues and received new power in my life. However I had to wait almost a whole year before Desmond was convinced that I was to be his wife!

Many doubts began to arise in my mind. *Was he really my type? Had I really heard from God?* Moreover, he didn't appear to show any interest in me whatsoever. He seemed determined to live as a bachelor in order to be better suited, as he then believed, to spread the gospel.

I had already left university and thought the case was hopeless. Suddenly I had a phone call. It was Desmond asking if I would meet up with him in a park in Lisburn. As Desmond began to talk, I realised that he had spent a lot of time in prayer preparing for this meeting. In fact we ended up discussing marriage and agreeing it would be in two years' time to allow him a year to work beforehand as a civil engineer. It was hardly the conventional first date but then both of us had been prepared in prayer and in meeting together at student events over an academic year.

The one matter Desmond was keen to mention was that he had always believed he would be a missionary some day. Of course he wanted to see how I would react to that. I immediately asked the question

'Where?' and he became very vague and unsure.

'Maybe Africa? but I really don't know where at this stage.'

At first my heart sank. Darkest Africa was definitely not for the faint-hearted like me.

By this time, I was pretty sure in my heart of hearts that I was called to the Spanish speaking world and more specifically to Spain itself. Two years before I had spent a month in Málaga, staying with a missionary couple from Costa Rica. They were working with the well-known American missionary Daniel del Vechio. Another confirmation had come to me there when the wife told me she had had a dream of me returning to Spain later as a full time missionary worker. In those days I didn't really believe that God could speak through dreams and visions. However it made quite an impact on me, although I was still struggling about going back to that country to live. I had begun to take an active interest in missions working in Europe such as the European Christian Mission, the European Missionary Fellowship and the Belgian Gospel Mission.

With all my inner struggles, I decided the best answer was simply to tell Desmond that I too believed I was called to be a missionary and leave it there. 'Doubting Thomas' as I was then, I decided that if this calling was of God, He would somehow or other give Desmond a clear call to Spain.

On 24 July, 1969 we were married. There were two ministers, both of whom had a great love for Africa. The one who married us had spent many years as a missionary in Nigeria and at church had enthralled us with his many stories from that period of his life. In fact he said he had had the opportunity to see and experience all the miracles recorded in the book of Acts, including the raising of the dead. We felt very privileged to have such a man marry us and instil in us a passion for church planting. He had planted a thousand churches with his team of three apostles and three prophets.

Our three-day honeymoon was spent touring in Southern Ireland. Then Desmond had to go back to work as a civil engineer in Londonderry, Northern Ireland. He suddenly came up with what was to be his passion for all our married life, evangelism. He had previously helped in evangelistic campaigns in Muirkirk, in Ayrshire, Scotland. His ex-minister was now serving there in the local Presbyterian church (Church of Scotland) so we set off for Scotland. We were staying with folks he knew but I didn't and the programme was hectic. I was thoroughly miserable and inwardly fuming but couldn't explain why. Of course years later we can laugh about how foolish we were to start off married life with an evangelistic campaign. As we have sought to prepare many others for marriage we have used that as an example of how not to begin married life.

Eventually our new bungalow was finished. My father, his cousin and I packed the wedding presents, including some furniture, carefully into a trailer hooked onto his car. We arrived at the door of this brand new bungalow one Friday afternoon. Desmond was frantically brushing out the dust and dirt while the builders were finishing, only to tell us that they had not been able to connect the electricity to the house. Nor could they do so all weekend. We looked at one another and suddenly living by candlelight seemed positively attractive to us. Above all we wanted to begin our married life together in a home of our own and nothing could stop us now. That first weekend was an adventure. We cooked on a simple two-ring camping gas stove. A lack of electricity didn't prevent us inviting a visitor back for Sunday lunch. This was the beginning of many visitors to our home for meals in the future.

Desmond had been made an elder in our church in Belfast before our marriage and found himself as the only elder helping a pastor now in Londonderry. This pastor had more than one congregation to attend to. Shortly after we joined the church, his marriage got into difficulty and his wife demanded a divorce. We were shocked, as was the congregation. He was so emotionally distraught that he could hardly function as a leader. We quickly found ourselves acting as pastors, although recently married and without any real preparation for the role. All this meant very much training on the job and we had to learn fast. One thing we did learn from that sad situation was that a pastor does need to take time out for his wife and family. If not there are consequences for all concerned. It was a good warning for us.

Much to our surprise Desmond was elected President of the North-West branch of the Graduates Fellowship in Northern Ireland (the Graduates section of the Universities and Colleges Christian Fellowship). This meant a lot of travelling to meetings and we were very young compared to the others in the group. At times it was quite daunting and too intellectual and we felt rather out of our depth. No doubt we made mistakes but the older folk were always so gracious. This again was good training for our future. We were able to follow that model. In Spain we gave many young people a chance to minister, even though they made mistakes.

FIRST JOINT VISIT TO THE IBERIAN PENINSULA. Our friends, Noel and Sandra Quinlan, had moved to Portugal to plant churches so we arranged to spend a holiday with them. Holiday was hardly the word as we raced around to one meeting after another in Lisbon and Sintra. However we were able to see and experience a model of church planting in the Iberian Peninsula. Sintra is often described as the Disney land for grown-ups. It was only in later years when living on the Portuguese border in Spain that we could visit those places again and appreciate all the beautiful architecture and history. One lovely young girl called Isabel caught our attention. She spoke perfect Spanish, having been brought up on the border of the two countries, and wanted to go to a Bible College in the UK. We decided on our last night that we should invite her to live with us for a year so that I could teach her English. The invitation came as no surprise to her.

'I had a dream last night that I was living with you in Northern Ireland', she told us.

Isabel came to be part of our family and during that time we learnt a lot about the life, food and culture of the Iberian Peninsula. It was largely her influence that made Desmond think about going to that part of the world. When he first mentioned it to me he heard the full story how I believed God had prepared me to serve Him in Spain.

DANGEROUS DAYS IN NORTHERN IRELAND. By this time I was pregnant but that didn't prevent us attempting some daring projects in Londonderry, at that time a very dangerous city. During the first year of our marriage, we heard a bomb go off there every single day. At night we were often awakened by our bed shaking. We had bought ourselves a new bright orange Volkswagen Beetle. A few months later it was parked outside the Guildhall building in the city centre where Desmond worked. A bomb damaged the car, filling it with tiny pieces of the beautiful stained glass windows of that famous building. Nonetheless we were grateful that no one had been injured. A university friend had been in a dress shop when a similar bomb exploded nearby and lost her leg as a result.

'Lie down.' shouted a British soldier. On more than one occasion we had to lie low in our car when crossing the main bridge into Londonderry. This bridge was controlled by British soldiers. They were often being shot at by snipers from the republican side of the city so we were in the line of fire. Prayer became very meaningful when we had to stretch out on the floor of our church building at one time in the city's main square. A bomb had exploded just across the street. In such moments, as you can imagine, everyone cries out to God, wondering if the end has come.

When a bomb explodes it makes everywhere shake in the surrounding area and one becomes rather used to lying down just in case the walls would cave in. In fact they did in our church building one Sunday evening about fifteen minutes after we had left it. That made us shudder but realise too how we were being protected. Psalm 91 and all its promises to guard us against danger became my favourite scripture in those days. All these experiences came in useful when we began to receive Colombians in Badajoz who had suffered from the rebel groups there and had to come into Spain as political refugees. They immediately felt they could relate to us. When the earthquake (5.1 magnitude) happened in Lorca, Spain in 2011, we felt a small tremor where we were then living. That seemed very small compared to the many tremors we had experienced in Londonderry.

I was teaching in some of the roughest areas of Londonderry and some of my pupils ended up in gangs and later in prison. We were very involved in a united church youth project called 'The Plaice'. This proved to be our first experience of a real move of God. Several hundred young folk were converted and this spilled over into the schools. I can remember how one fourteen year old pupil came running to me on my way out of school and saying

'Miss, Miss, what can I do to be saved?'

I was reminded of the story of Philip and the Ethiopian eunuch in Acts 8 and it wasn't just any normal fourteen year old pupil. It was one of the worst!

We then began to have children's and young people's meetings in our home with as many as eighty in our small lounge. They even wrote on the walls but we simply painted over it and continued. We had youth camps too and were excited by the many conversions and folk growing in God. I moved to teach in a new school and on my own began a Scripture Union meeting at lunch time once a fortnight in my classroom. Again that became very popular and up to a hundred teenagers would crowd in. It wasn't easy for me as they rushed out at the end almost knocking one another over so I had to leave my desk and stand at the door to keep a little bit of order. On one occasion my diary was on my desk and was stolen in the rush. The pupil who stole it then began to phone me each day after school, claiming to be the IRA (Irish Republican Army).

'I am ringing to warn you that I am going to kill you. We are coming to get you. You will not escape' was one such conversation.

I had my suspicions as to who it was but in that political climate it did make me very afraid. Neither the headmaster nor I were ever able to prove anything. The phone calls continued for weeks and were very wearing.

Years afterwards my husband confessed to me a threat that he had received which was even more real. As a civil engineer working in the 'Bogside', a very Republican area of the city, he had to dismiss some workmen. They attacked him, again threatening him with the IRA. His boss took the threat very seriously and took him off the job at once. He said he doesn't know how he managed to hide the bruises from me. At least I was spared all the anxiety that came from the incident.

Despite all these incidents we decided to show an evangelistic film *The Cross and the Switchblade* by David Wilkerson, in the Bogside, where the police didn't even dare to enter. Various young people agreed to help us. However, one by one they made excuses and only ourselves and the music band remained. It was just before our baby was due and I had fully intended to be present at the event. Desmond came back from setting up the hall and I noticed his face was rather white. They had offered to show him where they kept the illegal arms. If they had realised he was in favour of British rule in the country, he could have been in serious trouble.

'Darling, I don't really think you should join us tonight' was his comment so although very disappointed, I took his advice. All these experiences were preparing us for church planting in Spain.

A CHILD AT LAST. A few days later our son Michael Andrew was born, on 9 May 1974.

Having a baby brought us a lot of joy. A week after the birth we had a special visit from two of the Lutheran Mary Sisters working with Basilea Schlink in Darmstadt. We had arranged the meeting because of their emphasis on forgiveness and unity. These two elements were so needed in our very divided city of Londonderry. I still remember how they sang in our home and prophesied at the same time over our newly born son.

'This child will bring you a special joy' they said and indeed he already has on many occasions. So what next?

5 A BIT OF DANISH PASTRY

OFF ON A NEW ADVENTURE. Now that we were both convinced we were called to Spain, we decided that the time had come to sell our house. Were we foolish selling it at under market value so that the Salvation Army could buy it for their Captain? We were so keen to have the Christian influence remain that we took the lowest offer. Desmond had excelled himself in his job and was earning, at age twenty nine, the average salary of a forty year old civil engineer.

We bought ourselves a Volkswagen campervan which had a roof that opened up to make two bunk beds. We weren't very sure how we were going to get to Spain or Portugal or which of the two countries we should choose. At least we would have somewhere to live and our baby would have some space in the van to play while we travelled. Desmond had applied for engineering jobs in both places but the only offer he received was a job in Mozambique which didn't inspire us. We knew that was not our destiny so we decided to go to Bible College.

Desmond was very conscious that he had never been to Spain nor indeed visited much of Europe compared to me. For this reason he wanted to attend a Bible College outside the UK. After looking at several, Kolding Bible College in Denmark was our final choice. It offered all the lessons in Danish with translation into English, French and German which really attracted me. God spoke to us through the story of Abraham, Genesis 12:1 'leave your country, your people and your father's household and go to the land I will show you'. We were going out as he did, not knowing exactly where we would end up but with lots of faith. Was it presumptuous to leave family and home as modern day Abrahams? Little did we know that we would also experience something of the blessing mentioned in verses two and three in that same chapter. We were in fact to become a blessing to others in the Spanish speaking world.

BIBLE SCHOOL IN KOLDING, DENMARK

TWO DANISH CHILDREN AND MICHAEL AT KOLDING BIBLE

We had to leave our home ready for the new owners three weeks before our departure date. This meant we stayed with three different families with our one-year old son before departing from Northern Ireland. All these moves in the space of three weeks didn't bother me much and was good preparation for the many moves I was to have in Spain. For us it was all a big exciting adventure but not for our parents. They were so aware that we were giving up two good careers and had to bid farewell to their first and only grandson just beginning to speak. As we boarded the ferry in our new van I watched my father's tears as he saw us off. The farewell was painful and sad for all of us. I believe that not enough honour is given to the parents of missionaries who are also making a big sacrifice. *Were we wise leaving good well paid professions to follow our dream? Was it right to head off into the unknown on our own, instead of joining a recognised missionary society?* These and many other questions were in our minds as we set off. But God was guiding us on this journey.

LIFE AT BIBLE COLLEGE. It was now September 1975 and we arrived at the large impressive building in Kolding that was to be our home for that academic year. It was a modern four storey building overlooking a beautiful lake in its own grounds. How would we handle living in one small room with a very active one year old child?

As well as a hundred students in the Bible College, it also housed a Christian secondary school for boarders from all over Denmark. This was my first introduction to Christian schools. When we arrived, I was completely against isolating Christian children in what for me was a 'Christian ghetto environment.' However during the year, I had a chance to talk to many of the teachers and parents, who explained why they wanted this sort of education for their children. They explained how many rebellious teenagers were transformed into passionate Christians. I was eating in the same dining room as these teenagers every day. Again I was aware it was not by chance that I was at this particular Bible College for Christian Education was to play a significant role in my life.

As students we had to do an hour's practical work each morning from 6.00 am. This did not appeal to the two African students who were asked to clear away the ice from the lake so that folks could skate on it. Here I observed my husband's pastoral skills in action as he encouraged those Africans each morning. They became good friends as did a young Italian lad. He had been studying for the Catholic priesthood just before his life was turned around and he was suddenly in this strange environment. As the only Italian in the college, he so missed being able to converse in his own language. He then began to speak for hours to our son. By this time Michael had forgotten all his English since finding himself at our meal table listening to such a mix of European languages. He simply repeated whatever sound he heard. Each morning he was looked after by a Danish girl along with two other Danish children of his age whose parents were studying there like us. He eventually began to speak Danish which we didn't realise until someone stopped us on the stairs.

'Don't you realise, your son is trying to communicate with you?' we were told.

We had got so accustomed to his normal babbling mixture of languages that we didn't realise he had now settled down to speak Danish. We were in Denmark and his friends at nursery were speaking Danish.

I was allowed to look after Michael in the early mornings but had to do my practical work at midday while other students were resting. At times I felt very sorry for myself and had to battle with self-pity and resentment. My job was to clean along the skirting board and around all the doors, a very monotonous job which took me months of work to finish the whole building. It was a good lesson in perseverance which I often needed when dealing with difficult cases in Spain.

The course was very practical and not too academic, in fact an ideal preparation for missionary work. Bringing up an active toddler as three of us lived in one small room was not easy. He was constantly escaping running down the corridor or into someone else's room. In this way we made friends with a sixty year old German lady who had decided to come to the college on retirement. At times Carola felt out of things and under pressure with all the studies so she was delighted to entertain Michael on such occasions. Fortunately the staff saw our predicament and after Christmas decided to let us live in a small flat outside the college grounds. We shared a common lounge with the two other Danish couples who had young children.

During that year we made many new friends and we shared our dreams with one another. We had outings to other parts of Denmark and there saw the amazing sight of the frozen Baltic Sea. Our visit to Copenhagen was quite a memorable occasion. We visited the Royal palace and that famous bronze statue of 'the little Mermaid.' Perhaps more memorable for me was the visit to what was then called the city of 'Freedom and Love'. It was a part of the city where the police didn't enter as drug addicts had taken it over. The graffiti was all about freedom and love but the inhabitants seemed to be living in poverty and squalor. The atmosphere was dismal and typified an absence of freedom and love. I had little experience of drug addiction at this stage but knew enough to know that Christ is the one to give us both. 'You shall know the truth and the truth shall make you free.' John 8:32.

FEAR OF SPEAKING IN PUBLIC. While in Copenhagen we visited a very large church led by two outstanding men, Johannes Facius and Johnny Norr. The former became quite a famous intercessor who travelled all over the world in his ministry. The latter was famous in London some years later for organising the Festival of Light. Each time we visited a church during the course, some of the students were invited to give a testimony but I never expected to be speaking in front of such a huge audience in this large thriving church. Trembling, I said what I could.

At least I hadn't gone completely white as I used to in university when just reading out the treasurer's report of the Christian Union. It was progress. I remember once a social worker student said to me

'Caroline, just to watch you speaking in public makes me nervous.'

I thought to myself *you're not much of an encourager and yet you are preparing to be a social worker* but I didn't dare say it.

27

Someone who did encourage me a lot at university was Lord Mawhinney. He was then a student known to us as Brian and he later became Northern Ireland Minister of State. After that he entered the Cabinet and went on to be Chairman of the Conservative Party. Even in his university days, he was a 'mover and shaker' and somehow delighted in finding shy young Christian students whom he believed in (when we ourselves didn't!) and pushed us forward for the Christian Union committee. Committee work was all good training for my future work. Years later I did meet him and was able to thank him for that.

HOW TO GET TO SPAIN? By now we were beginning to question how we were going to get to Spain. One morning our German friend Carola came skipping into the lecture theatre, almost incoherent. She was very excitedly waving a magazine in front of our eyes.

'I knew this would happen', she exclaimed.

She was a woman of prayer and had been praying for us a lot. Now her group of churches were advertising for a couple to go to work with some German missionaries in Spain. She persuaded us to apply, which we did, only to receive a disappointing response. It was a German couple they were looking for, who could relate to the German churches. Believe it or not, the man who had put in the advert came to visit the Bible College six months later. No German couple had applied and he was now desperate, visiting the college in the hope of meeting a suitable couple. Their nationality was no longer so important. As he interviewed us, his first words were ,

'The British way of doing church is so different to the German way. I really wonder if we can work together in Spain.'

Our church in Northern Ireland had sent us off to Bible College with their blessing, although they said they couldn't actually commission us to go to Spain. The denomination we then belonged to parcelled out missionary destinations between different countries which had a sufficient number of churches to support such an initiative. The UK church didn't send missionaries to Spain; that fell to Germany. Here was the second hurdle. This gentleman said he would be happy for us to go to work with this

German family who wanted help but he couldn't help us financially as we weren't known to these German churches. We were happy with that as we still had the message of Abraham strong within us and we set off for Spain, calling at Darmstadt, Germany on our way. There we enjoyed a few days with the Mary Sisters who encouraged us greatly and gave us the first ever plaque of theirs for Spain. This was to be put in some place of natural beauty where tourists would see it and hopefully remember their Creator.

Little did we know the drama and the pain that awaited us.

Cordoba

6 THERE AT LAST! THE LAND OF THE MATADOR

FIRST IMPRESSIONS OF CÓRDOBA. On 9 May 1976 we arrived in Spain and celebrated our son's second birthday at the campsite where we had spent the night. This was Desmond's first glimpse of Spain. He remarked on all the new sights and sounds which were already more familiar to me after several visits as a student. However this was my first time in Córdoba and immediately I began hearing about 'El Cordobés', the famous matador. I had once been to a bullfight in Barcelona. The ear of the bull, covered in blood, landed beside our seats.

'Help, what do we do now?' I whispered to my university friend.

We decided to get out as soon as possible despite the deafening cheers of the crowd and their jumping up and down. It was extremely difficult to escape and I had no desire to see another bullfight. It was a big relief when the government many years later decided to ban bullfighting in the north of the country.

Córdoba with its population of some 350,000 was one of the most important capitals in Europe during the eleventh century. For a brief period of time Jews, Muslims and Christians lived peaceably together. Important philosophers, scientists and artists emerged from there such as Maimonides. Among the Jews Maimonides was considered to be a second Moses. He helped the Jews understand the Torah. Most people will have heard of the famous 'Mezquita'. This mosque with a Christian cathedral built in its heart has been described as the most beautiful and original building of all Spain. Busloads of tourists visit it all year round. It shows a mixture of different architectural styles as it was built and modified over nine centuries. When the Christians re-conquered the city in 1236, they consecrated the mosque to be the Christian cathedral. We were to spend the best part of the next eight years in this city.

The Jewish quarter of the city with its well-preserved synagogue is also worth a visit. Once there was a thriving Jewish community there. Many will have heard about the terrible suffering of the Jews in Spain and indeed this was the case. However not so many will have heard about the important ceremony carried out in Toledo in 1992. The King of Spain publicly asked forgiveness of the Jewish people. In fact many Spaniards have Jewish connections. We personally knew some of the group of intercessors who had prayed fervently for years for that event to take place. No doubt a difference happened in the heavenly realm when a monarch recognised the wrongs done against God's chosen people, the Jews. In fact in 1992 there were only around 40,000 evangelical believers in the whole of Spain. At the time of writing that had risen to one and a half million. Many of these have come of course from vibrant South American churches.

Córdoba is full of history. The main square has a statue of the great Captain Fernández (fifteenth century), famous for his service to the Catholic Kings of Spain and for his saying

'Hay que ser valientes; de los cobardes nada se ha escrito' (you must be brave; nothing has been written about cowards).

This was often a good message for me! The river Guadalquivir that flows through the city was where many Christians were thrown to the crocodiles during the Roman period.

Our first home was a flat above the church in Córdoba. The German family with their five children shared another flat just across the corridor, so our son played happily with them and was soon speaking German. Eventually he settled down to only Spanish and English but it never ceases to amaze me how children pick up foreign languages so easily.

CULTURE SHOCK. I will always remember our first outing with the church to the country. This is a very typical activity of the Protestant churches in Spain during spring or autumn months. The men were making a rice dish, which was the Córdoba equivalent of the Valencian paella while the women did all the preparation and of course the washing up. What we didn't expect was that the meal was only served at five o'clock in the afternoon, by which time we were very hungry. Of course we learnt with time that it is important to eat the many 'tapas' that are offered beforehand.

I was looking forward to a nice sweet dessert and horrified to find myself eating instead a cold tomato soup, called 'gazpacho'. While I came to appreciate all the varieties of this Spanish soup, I never really got used to eating it as a dessert when my palate demanded something sweet. Our own traditions are strong and hard to break. Desmond however was more disciplined. He did not like olives yet saw that we were constantly being offered them. So as not to offend, he decided he would train himself to eat one a day. It worked and now olives are one of his favourite foods.

At that stage some gypsy families who were attending the church also came to the outing. Soon they left us to form their own gypsy church, part of the *Filadelfia* movement that became the largest denomination in Spain, but more of that in chapter 24. I did have problems that day with some of their habits. Their children did not wear nappies so you can imagine the scene as our son ran around with them. My stomach turned inside out and I remember praying *Lord, make me tougher*. It took a while to answer that prayer but by the time I began our trips to Latin America (see chapter 23) I realised God had answered it. Most folk have stomach upsets at one time or another with all the strange food in those countries but I'm glad to say, I never did.

The footpath was so narrow on the street where we lived that it was quite dangerous with my pushchair each time I went out shopping. It all became quite stressful and I remember one experience when a bar owner and his friend pulled me into their bar just beside the church building.

'We know you English girls', they jeered 'you are here to have fun with some Spanish man'.

I was so shocked as they must have seen me regularly with our son in the push chair. They tried to caress me and I gave them the biggest smack I could and ran out.

My long auburn hair caught people's attention in Spain and I had to get used to all the shouts of 'guapa!' (pretty one) in Spain. Again I was living in a very different culture and I had to accept their customs, whether I liked them or not. Another strange custom was after the communion service in church. I discovered that they were giving the rest of the wine to the children, including our son. They assured me it was harmless sweet Malaga wine!

The pace of life in Spain is generally slower but that is the only way to survive in the heat. Tourists normally go to the coastal areas which have a very pleasant climate but in Córdoba the summer temperature was anything up to 45 degrees. Because of that shops in summer tend to shut between 2 and 5pm while most folk have the famous siesta. Meal times are later: between 2 and 3pm for lunch which is the main meal of the day. Supper is a slightly lighter meal and usually served after 9pm. It wasn't easy to make all these adjustments to our lifestyle but we knew there was no alternative. We had read enough missionary biographies to know that we simply had to adapt. We had come to love, serve and help and not to bring over our customs and traditions. Moreover when we wanted to put our son to bed, Spanish families were taking their children out for a walk in the cool of the evening.

Instead of being offered coffee and cakes at a Spaniard's home we were offered beer and savoury snacks. I absolutely hate beer but had to try to drink it. Sometimes we were given tea as they thought they were giving us a special treat. This could even include Earl Grey tea which is definitely not one of my favourite teas. Today I find it hard to understand the fussiness of the British about their tea. If they had been offered it as many times as I have been in both Spain and Latin America, they would be able to drink it in any shape or form; weak or strong, lukewarm but never hot, with lemon perhaps but never with milk!

Spaniards will not often invite people to their homes. They prefer to invite them to a bar. At first I was horrified at all the papers on the floor in the bars but then I learnt that that is what makes a good one. It simply proves that it is a popular one and will be cleaned each evening. Spaniards will appear to have so many friends as they greet so many in their local bar. However, only a few of those intimate ones are ever invited to their homes. They are very warm in their dealings with others wherever they meet and love to touch and kiss. We had to learn that and indeed un-learn it when we got back to the UK. In fact they come so close that it is off-putting at first to us Brits. They seem to be invading our personal space!

We began to hear more and more the famous word 'mañana' and got very frustrated at the lack of urgency in Spanish shops and businesses. Julio Iglesias, the famous singer, was once asked about the meaning of that word when interviewed on TV. His answer was the following

'Maybe the job will be done tomorrow, maybe the next day, maybe the day after that, perhaps next week, next month, next year, who cares?'

CONTRASTING THE REAL SPAIN WITH THE COAST. The German pastor decided to take us on a two day trip to visit some other English missionaries on the Costa del Sol. He thought it would be helpful and inspiring for us to talk to them just two weeks after we had arrived. Avril and Peter Hall lived in a beautiful spot just across the road from the beach. They had a community of various nationalities living with them and it all seemed so idyllic. In fact each time we go to that part of Spain we love it but realise it is far from the real Spain that God had called us to. We had to return from there with heavy hearts back to the reality of inland Spain and all its challenges.

COPING WITH LOSS. No one had ever taught us how to cope with loss. The average church member may have to cope with losses of different kinds during their life-time. For example loss of family through death or separation, loss of job, or financial loss. As missionaries by going overseas we choose to lose family, friends, country and culture, prestige or success as the world sees it. We also lose home and possessions, a 'normal education' for our children and a vibrant church around both them and us. We were learning how to cope with loss. We benefited a lot from a missionary retreat at Pinos Reales near Madrid that we attended shortly after our arrival in Spain. There we learnt from experienced missionaries and received their valuable orientation course for new missionaries. One elderly British Brethren missionary advised us,

'Don't insult the Spaniards by refusing their wine, in moderation of course. It is part of their culture.'

35

We both listened carefully and took note. Very soon we were to have a change of location.

7 PUTTING ON OUR L PLATES

YOUTH WORK IN A NEW TOWN After a few months Desmond went to help in an evangelistic outreach in Andújar. This is a town of 30,000 inhabitants in the province of Jaén, about an hour's journey from Córdoba. The outreach was organised by John Blake and his Billy Graham organisation called *Decision* along with *The Pocket Testament League*. There, about thirty young people made a profession of faith and the Spanish pastor pioneering a church in that town asked us to come and live there to help with the follow-up. We did this in August 1976, living at first in the camp-site until we had found a suitable flat in the town. We had found what seemed like the perfect flat. Then we said we were Protestants helping with the only Protestant church in the town. The owners flatly refused to let it to us and I was bitterly disappointed.

However I had to learn how it was in Spain: there was a real fear of anything not Catholic. We are talking about 1976, just one year after General Franco's death. This dictator had ruled Spain from 1939 until 1975 and had instilled a lot of fear into the people. He had used the Catholic religion as a social force to unite the strongly divided country. Protestants were labelled as 'heretics' and an undesirable 'sect'.

I had had an experience of that fear myself when at university. I had done a month's Spanish course with a friend at Barcelona University. We stayed with a couple from a large Brethren church in Madrid and went around with their young people's group. At weekends they handed out tracts, even though it was against the law in those days. They weren't even allowed to have a sign outside their churches. The young people warned us of what might happen if we were caught and we were told

'Just run as fast as you can if a policeman is in sight.'

I only helped them once and prayed a lot, needless to say, for my safety but these young folk were very brave and did this most weekends. I was very impressed.

The owner of the flat already mentioned was an English teacher and asked me for English lessons. I had to forgive the dear lady even though our next flat was not as nice and she often turned up for the class an hour late. When I spoke to her about this she said

'Everyone understands in Spain if we arrive late: something else has simply cropped up'.

Again I was learning to be patient and to accept that different cultures have different values. One redeeming factor at the end of that year was that she and her husband invited us to their lovely home for a sumptuous meal. She again apologised as to why they hadn't let us their flat. It seemed as if she had decided we were normal people after all and was feeling just a little bit guilty about her treatment of us when we first met!

Once we moved, we had visits very afternoon from lots of young folk asking endless questions about our faith. Desmond had learnt some Spanish up to then with the Linguaphone course but I had to interpret mostly for him. This was very unusual for the Spanish men who often laughed, saying

'This poor man cannot speak for himself and has to let his wife speak for him'.

I was rather annoyed by this male chauvinism which I hadn't come across in the UK. Moreover I had tried to teach him Spanish while living in Northern Ireland but had failed at the attempt. Determined that he should learn as fast as possible, I went out each afternoon with our son in the pushchair and left him to it. My excuse was that our super-active son cooped up in a flat needed some exercise.

We soon realised Desmond needed to concentrate more on language learning so he went off to Madrid for a month's intensive course. Some of the young folk later admitted

'We understood very little of Desmond's replies but something or other attracted us so we kept on coming'.

At times his lack of Spanish was very frustrating for him but we both prayed a lot into this, knowing that he was not a natural linguist. He had had real difficulties with French in school. Soon we saw an answer and he was preaching in the language much sooner than most foreign missionaries. In fact Spaniards will still congratulate him on his grasp of the language and especially on his use of a more cultured Spanish. He never tired of learning Spanish proverbs and sayings and throwing them into his sermons. We are both very aware that God really gave him the ability to fit the task.

THE GENEROSITY OF THE SPANIARDS. With Desmond in Madrid, I had an ideal opportunity to get to know my new neighbours. As I often did in Spain, I admired their plants on the balcony and was soon given generous cuttings from which to grow my own. They were very curious as we were one of the only two foreign couples living in the town. Tourists rarely came through that area. Both of us had auburn hair and our son as well in contrast to the usually darker hair of the Spaniards so we had to get used to being stared at each time we went out on the streets. In fact many were so intrigued that they would stop to stroke our son's hair and even give him a sweet or small coin. That was our first experience of the great generosity of that nation.

That generosity sadly does not extend much towards the clergy. We heard a lot of criticism about how the priests lived so well. Once people got used to the fact that Protestant pastors were married and often had to have a job apart from the church work, they were quite impressed.

PREPARING A CHURCH BUILDING. The Spanish pastor, Celedonio Martínez Pérez, his wife and two teenage children were supported by churches in Germany and began a church in their home. When we arrived Desmond started the heavy work of preparing a church building along with the pastor who fortunately was a very practical man. In Spain this is not what we normally think of as a typical church building. It is usually the ground floor of a block of flats which the builders have left completely bare. This is why Protestant churches are not easily noticed. The door could simply be leading into an office or shop. Floors and windows have to be installed as well as plumbing and electricity. Many comment today how Desmond is so practical but he learnt it on the job and reading lots of manuals.

SPANISH FAMILIES. Our year spent with Celedonio and his family taught us much about Spanish families. I admire their closeness and care for one another, especially for the grandparents who are much more respected than in our British culture. In fact, there is still a high percentage of homes in which family members of several generations live together. At times however the grandparents can have too much influence and spoil the marriage relationship of a son or daughter. They have not been taught much about 'leaving and cleaving' (Genesis 2:24)

We were taught at the very beginning 'Go for whole families,' and that was good advice for Spanish families have so many celebrations. If only one in the family wants to go to church on that occasion, it is very difficult for them. Not only does each Spaniard celebrate his/her birthday but also his/her saint's day. Christmas is one long celebration beginning at Christmas Eve with the traditional meal followed by Midnight Mass, then New Year's Eve and finally 6 January to give presents as the three wise men did. That day is a special family celebration and on the previous evening a large float goes through the town with the three kings (the wise men) as they call them, dressed up and throwing out sweets to the children.

Angela, the pastor's wife, was a typical Spanish housewife who went out every morning to shop at the local market to ensure that everything was fresh for her family's meals. I came from a culture where we were used to buying in bulk and keeping things in freezers. To me it seemed such a waste of time queuing up in the market every day. In fact they didn't really have queues in those days. Instead folk pushed their way in where they could and there were often very heated arguments about whose turn it was. If a man appeared he was always served immediately no matter how many women were waiting. I was young and enthusiastically suggested to Angela that she became more European and changed her shopping habits. Looking back I realise that was rather cheeky and I did not need to try to change habits of a life-time, unless they were contrary to the Word of God. However she was very gracious and did not complain.

A PILGRIMAGE. Andújar is found at the foot of the 'Sierra Morena', an attractive range of mountains. It is famous for a yearly pilgrimage to a spot where the Virgin Mary supposedly had appeared. There are many images of the Virgin that are venerated

ANNUAL PILGRIMAGE TO THE VIRGIN DE LA CABEZA
ATTRACTS 1 MILLION PEOPLE EVERY YEAR

GIRLS IN TYPICAL FLAMENCO DRESSES READY TO ENJOY
THE FESTIVITIES AFTER THE PARADING OF THE VIRGIN

throughout Spain and special sanctuaries such as these or others well known such as Virgin de Rocío, Virgin de Montserrat, Virgin de Pilar and Virgin de Guadalupe. As curious foreigners we decided to join the crowds on that day, climbing up the mountains. Folks had come from far and near and there were almost half a million of them. What struck me was the party atmosphere; not that God is against us having parties. I am sure He wants us to enjoy ourselves but the problem was that many people used it as an excuse to get horribly drunk and then as always the worst came out.

There was no evidence of God's presence during the whole day and I felt sorry for the older folk praying there with their rosaries. They were obviously seeking God but did they find Him or experience Him there? I very much doubt it. I had a similar thought before as a student when visiting Montserrat near Barcelona. What made me particularly sad there was the number of women climbing in their bare feet, some cut and bleeding, in the hope that some relative would be healed. The worshipping of the Virgin Mary is important for the Spaniards and many have refused to come to our meetings because of that, even though they have had a clear conversion experience.

OPENING OUR HOME TO SPANISH YOUNG FOLK. We found a spot in those mountains beside a lake and we began to take some young people there to camp from time to time. That was enjoyed by all and especially our open-air Bible studies by the lake which were very new for them. Our flat became an open house with young people popping in at all times of the day but they did abuse our kindness at times. I remember one evening for example opening our fridge for supper only to discover that it was empty. Some young folk had just helped themselves to the contents.

On another occasion some money was taken from my purse. We had a good idea who the culprit was but no real proof to enable us to confront her. She was one of ten children belonging to a divorced schoolteacher in the town whom I had become friendly with. Her mother had started coming to our meetings and we did not want to trouble her. What impacted me was that a few days later I received money in a letter from Northern Ireland with the exact amount of money I had lost. Was God trying to teach me the Biblical truth that He is no man's debtor?

Most of the young people we had were from very working-class backgrounds. I was learning in those early days how Spaniards don't use the words 'please' and 'thank you' as often as we would. This can come across as rude by British or American standards. We were offering food and drinks to folk in our home and rarely heard a thank you. For example in a large crowd people may bump into you and not apologise because it is not considered rude. I started to imagine that if we had some more middle-class Spaniards, it would be different.

Imagine my delight when a young man arrived who was from a well-off family. At least he expressed the odd 'thank you' now and again. However he didn't stay long after he was converted. He seemed to be like the rich young ruler and told us he was afraid God was asking too much of him. I had to accept that the customs that we take for granted are not always the same in other countries. For example I had to remember that it is considered rude in Spain to yawn or stretch in public.

Our young people's meetings became very popular in the town. In fact we were the only group that offered any sort of competition to the local Communist party. The rumour went around that Desmond completely brainwashed the youth by laying hands on them. Once again we saw complete ignorance of any Biblical way of praying. In some meetings we experienced a real flow of the Holy Spirit as in the book of Acts.

We saw a few supernatural healings and on one occasion we had a young man called Stanley from Northern Ireland staying with us for two weeks. We were both busy receiving the young folk at all hours of the day in our flat and were completely unaware of his feelings. In fact he was feeling very out of things because of his inability to speak Spanish and relate to the Spaniards, though we were translating what we could. But of course God was aware of it and one of the young teenagers began to speak in other tongues. What she didn't realise was that she was speaking in perfect English and in fact giving a very comforting message to Stanley.

Some of the young people were baptised and became active members of the church, whereas others drifted away. Desmond also had the privilege of baptising Marcos, the pastor's son, as a teenager. He served God faithfully from then on in various roles, including that of pastor of a church for some years. We were learning a lot about the Spanish mind-set. The decision-making process is more prolonged and convoluted than with the British. A Spaniard may agree to do something but for him that is only the starting point. He prefers to keep his options open until nearer the time. Even in business, directors of a company will make an appointment to see you several weeks ahead but ring you a day or two beforehand to check if you are still available. There is a definite tendency to live 'al día' meaning from day to day and that longer term commitments are more difficult for them to assimilate.

WALKING BY FAITH. After a year the German pastor in Córdoba and his wife felt called to go and pioneer a work in another small town called Montoro, so we were asked to pastor the church they were leaving. By this time the churches in Germany had decided to support us with quite a generous monthly sum. Before that God had tested our faith. We believed He was asking us to give away the rest of the money that still remained from the sale of our bungalow in Londonderry. This we did and shortly afterwards we heard that we were going to receive that monthly sum. We had visited a few of these churches after a year in Spain so that they could get to know us. We were very aware that we were being 'examined' during that visit so we depended very much on God's grace and favour. In one church I was giving my testimony in German and when I finished people were convinced I was German. I assure you that that had never happened before or since. It must have been a special anointing given for the occasion. The challenge now to actually pastor a Spanish church was very great. Perhaps God knew we needed some encouragement.

Our decision to go back to Córdoba was one that produced some exciting consequences.

8 GETTING INTO OUR STRIDE

FIRST EXPERIENCES AS FULL-TIME PASTORS. Two pastors came from the supporting churches in Germany to hold a special ordination ceremony for Desmond. It was a simple ceremony in German and Spanish at which he was officially recognised as pastor.

The church was small and became even smaller when we announced an evangelistic campaign! This was the year 1977. Most were simply unable to imagine people wanting to join their church. The older members had experienced such persecution for their faith and were full of the stories of the Civil War and even cited the horrors of the Spanish Inquisition. In Córdoba there had been a thriving Protestant church which had a school as well but the Pastor and head of the school were both executed and the school and church closed down. Others were thrown into prison or persecuted in more subtle ways such as losing their jobs or having their families threatened.

The majority of the church members were poor and one elderly man had a problem with alcohol. During the first few weeks when Desmond was the new pastor this man came into a service having had too much to drink. He sat down beside me, threw his arm around me and continued like that for some time. I didn't dare throw it off in case he would make a fuss and we were in the middle of Desmond's sermon. Desmond saw him but didn't dare do anything either so I had to wait and pray until he finally tired and walked out again. The whole experience did leave me shaken and I wondered what sort of a church we had come to.

Early on a Sunday morning we heard a special warbling sound, rather like a whistle. That marks the arrival of a knife-sharpener in Spain. This one was Miguel, our church member, with his small dark wizened face. He would walk up our street wheeling his bicycle which he didn't seem to ever ride. Instead he used it for his tools to sharpen the knives brought by the housewives onto the street. I remember visiting his home. As I looked around it I reflected that it was more like an outhouse on my father's farm than a home. I was amazed that I was so happy sitting there and asking God how we could help Miguel and his wife. They couldn't read or write so we helped them fill in forms from time to time and did what we could to give them food. God was giving me a love for these people.

POLITICAL CHANGES IN THE LAND. King Juan Carlos, named by Franco as his successor, led the country through a process of democratic reform. In 1978 a democratic constitution was proclaimed guaranteeing basic civil liberties, including freedom of religion. At this time major social changes began to sweep through Spanish society. Moral taboos previously imposed by the Franco dictatorship were quickly dismissed. Traditional, right-wing Catholic Spain began to do an 'about-turn' or 'pendulum swing' as far as moral and religious values are concerned.

During the first few years there was a new openness as well to evangelical Christianity. Folks were curious about other types of churches so we went ahead with our campaign. The evangelistic campaign did bring in a steady stream of young folk whom we then discipled. The older folk who had 'gone underground' began to come back with new hope.

THE COST OF BEING DISCIPLES. Some of these new teenagers didn't have it easy with their parents. One girl, Marie Carmen, was beaten several times by her father to try to stop her coming to our church. However she persevered and it was a joy to see her almost forty years later when we recently visited Córdoba. Both she and her husband were battling with cancer but she hardly mentioned that; she just kept telling how God was blessing her and her family.

Africa is not an unusual name for a woman in Spain. This Africa was as bighearted as the continent itself. She suffered a lot from her husband for coming to our church. He had been an officer in the army and although retired still acted as if he was in the army at home. At times we thought he treated her more like a slave than a wife and he demanded she always be at home to wait on him.

BELLEWS c1977 CÓRDOBA CHURCH ENTRANCE

One particular Sunday she got back home rather later than usual from church and he was furious that he couldn't have his Sunday lunch at his usual hour. He tried to kill her with a knife but fortunately fell short and only slashed her face. She arrived at church that evening with this horrible gash, obvious for us all to see. Her face was marked until the day she died but that did not prevent her loving and serving him faithfully for years after that. He did finally become a Christian and softened a little after we had left the town. She was a real tower of strength to everyone in the church. When the church later became part of the Spanish Assemblies of God denomination, she was made an elder.

One time Desmond came out in large ugly lumps on his legs. The doctor was puzzled and decided he must have had TB when he was younger without realising it! The cure was going to be medication with so many side-effects that we were very uncertain about beginning it. Instead we called for Africa who knew how to pray effectively and the lumps soon disappeared.

This same lady prayed for our son too when he began school and seemed to pick up every infection that was going around. This was before Spain was part of the European Union so we had to pay for anything to do with health. Not only was God our best physician but He was also a lot cheaper! On the other hand we did see some remarkable healings in our churches when we prayed. Our son Michael loved to imitate his father and would also lay hands on people. On one such occasion when he prayed for Africa, she felt heat go through her whole body and was instantly healed.

BEGINNINGS OF COMMUNITY LIVING. Some of the young folk we were dealing with came from difficult home situations and they found it hard to accept that God really loved them. They wanted to follow God but their lives were sadly lacking in discipline. This led us to consider inviting some of them to live with us. Some came for short periods and some for longer.

One young man called Ignacio Zurrita with his head of long wild curly hair stayed with us for six years. His appearance spoke loudly of rebellion but it was understandable when we heard his story. As a young lad he had fallen off a horse in the country and broken his arm. The family were too poor and uneducated to do much about it with the result that gangrene set in. Eventually the arm was amputated. The father himself an alcoholic, had continually reminded him,

'You are absolutely useless, unfit for anything in this life'.

This led him to leave home, get into drugs and hang around with prostitutes. On one occasion he was back in his home town of Montoro and responded to the gospel shared by the German pastor there. In that small town he had no other young company and therefore it was agreed he should come to live with us in Córdoba.

He had had little schooling and could hardly read or write so we helped him with that. I can still hear him up in the flat roof of our house reading the Bible aloud to himself. With his one arm he attempted everything and wanted to learn from us. He even learned to cook. Each time I meet him and his wife, also converted with us in those early days, they still thank me for teaching him to cook and clean the house. He did a five month Discipleship Training School (DTS) in Madrid with YWAM and this helped him a lot.

We had to protect him a little as well. On several occasions one of his old prostitute friends came to visit him. It was a big temptation of course for him as she wanted him to leave and go off with her as before. She kept saying how much he had changed and how happy he now seemed. I tried to explain how it was God who had changed him and how He could do the same for her. She wanted to but kept repeating

'I couldn't, I couldn't!'

I still remember the pain on her face and how horrible it is to see women like her trapped in such a lifestyle. I was so disappointed that we couldn't see her freed but God heard my prayers. He allowed me to see others even worse than her come to know Him.

God had a good wife for Ignacio, Ana Marie; a timid young girl who arrived at our church at fifteen years of age. Rarely have I seen a teenager who was such a bundle of nerves and on so much medication because of that. After her conversion, she began to understand God's great love for her and His acceptance. It was thrilling to watch her change before our eyes.

After they were married, they both went to live at the drug addict centre where Ignacio was one of the first official helpers for several years. Later we often stayed with them and their two well trained sons, both in their twenties, when passing through Córdoba. It is such a joy to see them and realise the transformation in their lives.

We tried to provide a loving yet very disciplined atmosphere for these young men who had been mainly unemployed. The routine was to get up early for a quiet time before breakfast. This was a shock to the system as Spaniards are not used to early rising. Then it was an even greater shock when they discovered they had to make their own beds. They had always expected the women of the house to do that sort of thing.

Coming from traditional Spanish homes, chickpea stew and lentil stew were on the menu each week. These stews were made from cheap cuts of meat and full of fat and I had to learn how to cook them. However hard I tried, I never seemed to be able to cook them quite right for them and was sometimes in tears. Eventually my husband insisted

'There will be no complaints at the meal table and we have to learn to be grateful for whatever is put in front of us'.

Our turn came when they began their attempts at cooking for us all!

Two young men we had known in Andújar also came to live with us. Félix Valverde was only sixteen and was on the point of entering a seminary to become a Catholic priest. Instead he decided that he wanted to serve God as a Protestant one. He was a very good artist and enjoyed giving lessons to Michael our son. This was God's provision for me as I had absolutely no talent in that direction and had even less idea how to teach it. We had foreign groups come from churches in both Germany and the UK to help us and Felix fell madly in love with several of the young ladies. Then I was asked to translate these very romantic poems he would write for them. I was discovering the artistic and poetic ability which is very common among Spaniards. We have several

THREE CONSECUTIVE
PASTORS OF THE CHURCH
IN CORDOBA: (from right to
left) CELEDONIO (Spanish),
JUAN (German) & DESMOND
(British)

DESMOND BAPTISING
ONE OF THE EARLY
CONVERTS

of Félix's pictures in our home still to-day. Félix lived for several years with us and was a special favourite with us both, I must admit.

Years later we caught up with him again, only to discover that his marriage had broken up, he had lost a lovely home, became an alcoholic for a while, and was now dying with cancer. His only company seems to be his dog and his many pictures. He told us he still talked to God every night but sometimes wondered if He really heard him. What a sad ending for someone who started out well, planned to become a pastor but somehow got off course! He was now ending his life in disillusionment but wanted us to have one of his pictures. This he had signed on the back expressing lots of sentiments about our years living together. He claimed he still loved us more than anyone else and looked forward to seeing us again in heaven. Ministry to others brings both sadness and joy when we meet folks years later.

The other young man was Juan Carlos Expósito with his striking dark eyes. He was eighteen and struggling to give up smoking. He used to tell us so many times that he was free of it and when I was washing the blankets one day, I discovered a burn-hole in one of them. Juan Carlos had been smoking under the bed clothes, hoping that no one would discover it! Time and again we found him lying to us and his endless chatter really got to us at times when we longed for a little more quietness in our home. He reminded me of the joke about the four men having a conversation. If they are English, one speaks and the others listen. If they are Spaniards, everyone speaks and no one listens. This custom is not even considered rude but a shock for us British. Once he came to me, saying

'Carolina, I really think you don't like me for Félix is so obviously your favourite.'

I was discovering the extreme sensitivity of the Spaniards. We can't hide things from them and they are very easily offended. Nor can we overlook their feelings of inferiority as a nation. Juan Carlos was desperately trying to please us, to be accepted by these strange foreigners.

I was absolutely taken aback and didn't know what to say to him as I knew he was correct. I thought I had a real love for Spaniards but God was teaching me to cry to Him to receive more love for Juan Carlos. His love is unconditional. My patience was quickly running out and I realised how much I had to depend on God. 'The spirit indeed is willing but the flesh is weak' as we read in Matthew 26:41. The perseverance with him was really worthwhile.

His 'gift of the gab' came in useful when he started one of the first Christian radio stations in Spain. He has pastored several churches but his real gift is in evangelism. He is now the official evangelist of the Assemblies of God, travelling all over Spain and beyond to countries in Europe holding evangelistic campaigns and training conferences. He has also brought the churches in Córdoba together to do open air evangelism in the centre of the city. Indeed now we count it a real honour to have had him to live with us in those early years of his Christian experience. He is a stark reminder to us that God's purposes for his people are not always revealed to us. He has chosen to use him in ways we would never have imagined possible.

The church members watched how these young men changed under the discipline in our home. The bottom floor where we lived housed the church building and a kitchen with toilets and we lived on the second floor in a self contained flat. On the other side of the corridor were three bedrooms where the young men slept. At first the members expected the pastor and his wife to keep the church building clean. We had to teach them that the church was a body of people and all were meant to serve. It was a time of stretching for us in all senses of the word. Moreover I had just begun to home school our son. I realised God had given me a love for Spaniards but having them living in my house was a different matter. Many times I had to cry out to God to give me His love for each one of them.

The building had a large flat roof which was ideal for our son to run around. There he had his plastic paddling pool for the summer months when the temperatures could reach 45 degrees. Eventually the young men under Desmond's guidance built some sheds where they kept canaries, chickens and even turkeys. Not only did this teach them to work for the first time but it provided a little money towards their food. Now and again some of our church members would give them employment on a temporary basis.

VISITS FROM YWAM IN OUR CHURCHES. We first connected with YWAM when living in Londonderry. This is a large international mission that sends out more workers than any other mission in the world. When pastoring the church in Córdoba, we began to receive groups of DTS students from the Madrid base. The opening paragraphs of my book mention a group that came from YWAM Denmark. They would take over my kitchen and we enjoyed some very international cooking for a week or ten days. The groups were always very helpful in practical matters. We had a large building that always needed lots of repairs and, despite the endless energy my husband seems to have, we simply couldn't manage to do everything that needed to be done. International teams came to fill that gap.

Their testimonies were much appreciated by our church members and indeed they opened the eyes of our small congregation. They let them know that there was another world out there where our God was very much on the move. They were of particular encouragement to the young men living with us as they joined in their street evangelism. The directors in those days were an American couple named Bob and Vicky Lichty. Bob has unexpectedly gone to be with the Lord since I began this book. We often got a phone call warning us that Bob and Vicky were coming and might bring one or two friends as well. The 'one or two' often became five or six. It is such a joy to know that some of those he brought about forty years ago, to experience their first flavour of a Spanish church, are now the national leaders in YWAM Spain.

I did have difficulty with my household budget to feed so many extra mouths. Many times towards the end of the month, I would wander around the market where provisions were cheapest and pray about what to buy for the week. With having had such a generous father, I didn't find it easy to buy for as many as twelve people living with us at one stage on a tiny budget. There were many tears and reminding myself of Bible verses such as 'My God shall supply all your need' Philippians 4:19. I discovered that the cheapest meals were the stews already mentioned or fried sardines or clam soup. In fact for years after the young men left us I had had so much of those meals that I couldn't bear to think of eating them again or even making them. Desmond on the other hand missed those type of meals so much that he began to cook them for himself at times and put them into the freezer for use when I was away. I'm glad to say all those memories must have been healed because I can now thoroughly enjoy those traditional Spanish meals.

Little did I realise that our faith would soon be tested.

9. FROM FEAR TO FAITH

Our faith was tested as never before when we decided that God wanted us to trust him completely for all our needs. We renounced the salary from Germany which no-one else could understand. However we were convinced that God wanted us to take that step and we had already learnt the importance of obedience however great the cost. Although we had a good circle of friends and relatives in Northern Ireland who supported us from time to time, we were determined not to let them know our change of circumstances. It was exciting to experience God's provision in an even greater way in our lives. One thing I had asked God for was that I would never be in debt. That was a principle that my father had instilled in me.

On one particular Monday Desmond had given me the food money for the week and then said that that was the last money he had. There was nothing more in the house or in the bank! I was full of faith until a knock came to the door. There stood a man to collect money for our health insurance policy. I fumbled around not knowing what to say and then in a trembling voice asked

'Please can you come back tomorrow because my husband is in a meeting and can't be disturbed.'

He was actually in a team meeting with the German and Spanish pastors. By this time I was in tears, convinced that God had let me down and we were going to be in debt.

To my total amazement, after the meeting Desmond showed me a one hundred deutschmark note. The German pastor had been moved to give us that money, something he had never done before and never did again! It was the exact amount for the insurance policy. It was a real confirmation for me of God's faithfulness. I can testify that we have never been in debt, though sometimes on our last penny. What a wonderful God we have!

With time other young folk came from abroad to help out and they always paid us for their keep which was a great help. Also they were disciplined people who were a good example for the

YOUTH IN THE CORDOBA CHURCH

ALL AGES WORSHIP IN CORDOBA

young Spaniards. Fritz Hammershoj from Denmark came for two years, learnt Spanish and later moved on to Bogotá, Colombia. There he set up an impressive work with orphanages for street children.

Wendy Shepherd, a teacher from the UK came originally to help teach our son but only after a week or two, she and I decided she was more gifted than I was in cooking and she became instead the main cook. Both Wendy and Fritz have thanked us for the training they received with us and say that it was during that period that God called them to mission. Wendy actually joined up with a YWAM team visiting us that was on its way to Morocco. There and then she decided she was called to Morocco, not Spain and eventually went on to teach English there with the well-known mission Operation Mobilisation (OM). She is still there at the time of writing.

We will always be grateful also to another Danish couple who lived on the Costa del Sol. Albert Hansen was a carpenter and his wife Gyde kindly released him to come to stay with us from time to time. This couple had left their country with their four children in a Land Rover and caravan. Their destination was sub-Saharan Africa. They then decided that Spain was a needy mission field and never got to Africa. Albert helped us out with the many repairs constantly needed in the large older property that had been bought by the generous German churches.

The downstairs kitchen from the church looked over a patio and at times rats would come up from the sewers and dive into the kitchen if the door was open. Now the many new insects I came across in Spain never bothered me but rats, YES. I was frantically cleaning and disinfecting the whole kitchen in a bit of a nervous state. Ignacio simply couldn't understand what I was fussing about and told me

'My mother often had rats coming into her kitchen and never got alarmed'.

I realised I was dealing with a very different culture.

OVERCOMING FEARS. A couple who had recently come to the church from the Canary Islands asked us if we would keep their thirty-year-old son for two weeks while they had to go back to the island. What they didn't tell us was that this son Juan Antonio was an alcoholic. We soon learnt it ourselves when one day our three-year-old son disappeared for about six hours. God gave us a special portion of His peace on that day. Desmond decided to go around the bars in the area and eventually found them both in a nearby bar.

Michael, our son, had thoroughly enjoyed his 'pub crawl' and was being treated to orange juice and yoghourt, while his new-found friend was fast asleep! The two weeks in our home turned into two years and it was a long learning curve to know how best to help alcoholics. He seemed to be progressing and then we were disappointed when he fell again and went out on the town. One such occasion was when he climbed into our lounge one night as reported in the preface to the book.

Another night was very significant for me. He arrived in very late and slightly drunk. He looked me straight in the eye and said

'Carolina, you are afraid of me but there is no need to be. I would never touch you because there is too much of God about you.'

It was amazing how those words went deep down into me and from then on I was never afraid of drunk people as I had been for years. I was learning the reality of God as my protector in all circumstances.

Indeed I had lots of fears which had to be dealt with and depended so much on Desmond but he began to get invitations to minister in other parts. What was going to happen if there was a crisis among the lads and Desmond out of town? Moreover in the summer heat, we had to leave my bedroom window open and any of them could have climbed in. I used to lie awake in bed thinking about all the gory details of their sordid past life. My own life had been so innocent in comparison yet that is why they said they trusted us to confess their terrible past. Over the years God made me stronger and helped me to face my many fears and overcome them.

ONE FINAL ATTEMPT TO SHOW LOVE. Juan Antonio didn't fit in easily with the other young men in our home. To begin with, he was quite a bit older than they were. Spanish young men are very particular about their appearance and will use a lot of eau de cologne to make sure they smell good. Juan Antonio was the exception in those days. They came to the point that they told me they just couldn't wash his laundry in with theirs! We decided to make one last attempt to share God's love with him.

We moved our son out of his bedroom and gave it to him. I did his washing with our own and he was touched. Juan Antonio was transformed and married a young lady from our church. It was December 1979 and Desmond's first opportunity to perform a wedding ceremony. Just when they heard they were expecting their first child, he went to court for a previous offence from years back and was given a two-year prison sentence. This was a big blow to them but he served his time and came out all the more repentant. He took up sport and cycling in a big way and they enjoyed a happy marriage for about ten years. Then sadly he was killed in a cycling accident. When we heard we were glad to know that at least he had been freed from his terrible addiction and had gone to be with his maker. We were glad that we hadn't given up on him, though tempted to on many occasions.

LEARNING FROM YWAM. YWAM had plenty to teach us about community living. This came from years of strategies that were tried and tested in many countries and with many different cultures. We had only Spaniards and British in our home at a time and that led to quite a few emotional 'explosions', enough for us in any case. We also learnt about the practicalities of team and, the importance of loyalty to each other on the team. In other words there was no chatting behind backs by members of the same team. If a team doesn't have this principle in place, many hurts are caused unnecessarily. Indeed in the future we were to experience a lot of these hurts when working in another team context.

NEEDY PEOPLE. We began to take in other needy cases. We had lots of faith but looking back, not much wisdom perhaps when we took in a young schizophrenic man. This young man had attempted to kill his mother with a knife. He was extremely tall for a Spaniard. When he decided to threaten the other young men who were smaller with a large kitchen knife, in the middle of the night, it was not easy for them (this was another incident I referred to in the preface). They immediately called out for help and Desmond had to run on several occasions into the bedroom to calm down the situation. Thankfully he recognised Desmond's authority and always became quite docile though the young men were trembling and I was waiting in our own bed rather trembling myself.

With time, we realized we were not having any real success with him so we had to ask him to leave. He did this somewhat reluctantly and for several nights we had to lie in bed and listen to his knocks on the front door and screams outside our bedroom window

'Please, please, Ramón, Carolina, let me come back'.

I was equally determined not to have him back and pleaded with Desmond to ignore his cries, which I'm glad to say he did. I hope he went on to get the psychiatric care he needed.

I must explain at this stage why my husband was called Ramón and most folk then believe his name is Raymond in English. When he became pastor of the Córdoba church our good friend Paco (now Dr Francisco Javier González and member of our church at that time) became very concerned about using his English name in Spain. Francisco had just returned from a year's Bible course in Wales so people listened to what he had to say. Folk in Andalucía tend to leave out their 'S' and therefore DESMOND sounded like 'DEMON'. This was hardly an appropriate name for a pastor so he suggested RAMÓN and that name stuck with him after that.

The young men went out testifying in the streets and this brought more and more drug addicts and alcoholics to our door. News seemed to fly around that they would receive food or blankets to throw around them to sleep in our church porch. As my blankets started to disappear we had to be more careful. On one occasion our four-year-old son went to the door with Ignacio and they were threatened by a drug addict. He flashed a knife and pushed his way past them. I can't remember how the situation was resolved but once more we knew God's faithful protection.

A STRIKING EXAMPLE OF GOD'S PROVISION. I sometimes used to worry what the neighbours in our street were thinking of all the strange goings on in our home. The street was so narrow that they must have heard the noise many times. Fortunately Spaniards can put up with a lot of noise but I didn't realise that. One Sunday morning an irate Spaniard came to shout and scream for about an hour outside our door because his wife had started to come to our church. I was left rather shaken.

Much to my surprise a neighbour living across the road arrived to speak to us. She said she had noticed the good work we were doing with all these young men (she had even noticed Juan Antonio climbing up the window ledges to get into our lounge) and would like to help us by offering some furniture. In fact she offered us the entire furniture from a flat she was now renting unfurnished. We had all been praying with Ignacio for furniture as he was about to be married and move into unfurnished accommodation. This was a wonderful answer to our prayers.

DIFFICULT CHARACTERS. Another person we had was called José Louis. He came from a village near Huelva in South Western Spain and at age seventeen struggled with the discipline now established in our home as well as that from his own parents. We were invited once for a few days to another small town called Palma del Río so we decided to take him with us. Palma del Río had a population of 25,000 inhabitants. The invitation was to the home of a very wealthy lady called Pilar, who had been converted in Marbella along with her sister. Her husband was very opposed to her coming to our church so we could only see her when her husband was away on business. In fact several times he pointed a gun at her but dropped it when she prayed. He had a fleet of small aeroplanes which were used to spray crops and take aerial photos. At times they dined with the King and Queen of Spain, so an invitation to their house was something special.

I still remember the number of maids she had there, the large swimming pool and the beautiful guest room where we slept with its en-suite and choice of perfumes. These were more expensive than any I had ever used. José had his own bedroom and en-suite but he didn't appreciate it. Instead he got so angry that some Spaniards could live like that while he had come from such a poor family. However we tried, we were unable to calm him down and when we got up next morning, we discovered he had left and taken my guitar with him. Once more we experienced God's faithfulness. As we were driving home on the outskirts of Palma del Río we suddenly noticed my guitar in the ditch. His conscience had seemingly pricked him and he couldn't continue with the robbery. Fortunately it was dry weather and the guitar was barely damaged.

We never heard from him again until suddenly he walked into our church in Badajoz about twenty years later with his wife and two children. He had visited another church and told his story about stealing a guitar from these British missionaries in Córdoba. The pastor guessed it was us he was talking about so sent him to us. He was excited to meet up with us again and soon his wife and children became Christians. He asked our forgiveness as well as God's. For some years they struggled in and out of church and he was on a lot of medication for depression. We had to rescue both husband and wife at one stage as they each tried to commit suicide on separate occasions.

They moved to another church where two doctors, a husband and wife seemed to take an interest in them. He had to give up his job as a successful insurance salesman and eventually left that church as well. We were surprised to see them with their daughter and child at our farewell but saddened to think that they hadn't really let God change their lives. *Had we failed to help them for some reason or another?* This is always the question you have when people fall away.

Not all were success stories from those days. YWAM asked us to have a young Englishman to live with us. It was supposedly for a very short period as he said

'I am just waiting for money from England to pay for my fare home'.

He had been travelling as a hippy in Morocco and after his conversion there with YWAM he went to their base in Madrid. They had had problems with him but thought we, being British, could understand him better than those on the base at that time, who were mostly Americans.

He was extremely lazy and the weeks were going by and there was still no sign of this money according to him. Each morning he would escape when he could and go off into town. One day

Desmond decided to follow him as we began to suspect he was lying to us. He went into one of the most expensive cafeterias in town. In fact it belonged to an exclusive men's association where he could sit smoking cigars and read the newspaper in English, a rare happening in those days in Córdoba. According to others living with us he had been doing this for some days, if not weeks, and never giving us a penny towards his keep.

When we discovered he had been deceiving us we had to ask him to leave. He was furious because by this stage he had spent most of his money and no longer had the fare to get home.

Desmond advised him to go the British Embassy in Madrid where we knew he would get help to get back to the UK. However he was so furious that he took up an already opened pot of paint in our bathroom and simply threw it all around the place. That took us some hours to clear up. It was agreed that I should drive him to the outskirts of town and leave him there to hitchhike to Madrid. Desmond had another appointment which couldn't easily be changed. He refused to get out of the car and kept pleading with me about my cruel husband putting him out penniless. I was shaking and prayed as never before.

'You have to leave, you have to leave', I insisted.

He eventually got out but this time stood in front of the car so that I couldn't move. He was angry and capable of anything and I was completely at his mercy. I remembered my authority in Christ and continued to pray inwardly. It seemed a very long time but eventually he moved out of my way and I drove off as fast as possible.

We were learning that love has to be firm as well. We heard nothing for years and then one day perhaps twenty years later a fellow British missionary came to give us word of this same young man. He had met him at a meeting when on deputation work in England. The message he sent us was a big thank you for sending him home when he did. He said

'It was the best thing you could have done and because of that I really got myself sorted out as a Christian'.

What a relief to know that that hard experience both for him and for us had worked out for his good!

Another American couple were sent to us from YWAM. What we were not told was that their marriage was very shaky. Sadly we were unable to help this couple but it led us to realise the importance of regular marriage courses in churches and especially for church leaders. Later we introduced several. The last one we used in Spain was a translation of the Holy Trinity Brompton one (London) and this we found very successful.

UNITY WITH OTHER CHURCHES IN THE CITY. We had got to know the Baptist pastor in Córdoba as he had invited us to interpret for some of his American visiting preachers. This friendship led to a united prayer meeting for revival in Spain held by our two churches on 19 February 1978. We formed a real friendship among us all. On 14 May 1978 we then had our first joint meeting for all the churches in the building belonging to Salem (this denomination was led by Marcos Vidal, the famous songwriter and singer from Madrid). Sometime later we had the first joint ladies' meeting in the town when I was asked to speak on 'Bringing up children'. I remember feeling very inadequate for the task, with only one son while most Spanish families were so large. However God helped me as always in my weakness and one pastor's wife in particular was touched as she had tended to put her church work before her three children.

IMPORTANCE OF FAMILY TIME. I had had a strong warning about this a few months before. A German lady had come to visit us with her English husband. They were both very active in a growing church in Northern Germany. Imagine their shock to receive a phone call saying that their eighteen-year-old son had just been put into prison for murder. It was a serious drug related offence. The husband was so upset that he asked me to try and comfort his wife who was sobbing for hours while he dealt with his own grief. I must say this was one of the hardest tasks I had ever been given. They both kept repeating

'If only we had given our son more time and less time to the church people- if only, if only...'

For years I remembered their aching cries. Thankfully the boy did repent and was let out after a few years but I had learnt my lesson.

We made sure we took each Thursday off to be with our son. Since he had endless energy sometimes we took another boy to play with him. David Bea was the son of Angel Bea, another pastor in the city so they could relate to one another. David Bea is today a famous figure in the Spanish musical scene and has made many CDs and DVDs. There were never many children of Michael's age in our church so we had to make other arrangements. We received a Dutch lad once for a weekend who was the son of Jaap and Suze de Bruine or on another occasion he went to stay with their family in Madrid. Like us they were church planters and at one time also national leaders of Worldwide Evangelisation Crusade (later re-named WEC International).

PRISON VISITING. As a result of visiting Juan Antonio in prison, Desmond was able to begin meetings inside it. This was a great victory as other Spanish pastors had been refused permission and Desmond, though a foreigner, was soon given it. He continued once a week for about six years. We believed we were obeying Hebrews 13:3 'Remember those in prison as if you were together with them in prison.' One by one other prisoners were converted and when they were given parole they came to visit us in our home. Desmond later expressed how strange he felt to come home and find two prisoners who had been murderers playing happily with his son in our patio. Often he didn't tell me the background of these prisoners who came. They used to love Michael and made footballs and other toys for him in their craft classes.

It was a new experience for me to receive the mothers of these prisoners in our home as well. They had such sad stories to tell. In the short time I was talking to them, I would do my best to share the gospel and give them some hope for their broken lives. I only visited Juan Antonio once in prison and that experience was quite enough for me. He had to share a dormitory with so many other men and they kept pinching his soap, shampoo or toothpaste. Conditions were so spartan and I couldn't help but compare them with the conditions in an English prison. Years later we were invited to go to Portland Bill Prison several times to visit some Colombian drug criminals and have a meeting in Spanish. The conditions seemed almost luxurious in comparison. I am glad to say that we were pioneering a prison ministry in Córdoba. This was continued as a united project by all the churches in the city and still exists at the time of writing.

But what about our families?

10 FAMILY VISITS

DESMOND'S FAMILY. We always enjoyed visits from our family when living abroad. Desmond's father, when he came, was highly respected and appreciated and you could have heard a pin drop when he was preaching. That reflected the attitude to the elderly which is a characteristic of Spanish society and even more in Latin America. We were very conscious that he was on his own when his wife died and did offer for him to come to live with us. However we can understand his refusal to do so because the change of lifestyle at his age would have been difficult for him to handle.

Desmond's Aunt Maimie from Canada was another popular visitor. I remember my embarrassment on her first visit when I peeped into her bedroom. There she was in bed with her umbrella carefully placed above her pillow to protect her from the drips from the flat roof above her bedroom!

Aunt Maimie had been a captain in the Salvation Army and had never been in a meeting where the gift of tongues was used. She was convinced at first she had heard an angelic choir. Desmond had the unusual task of baptising her by immersion in our church in Córdoba. She was suffering a lot with her hand, which she couldn't open without a lot of pain. It was a case of Carpal Tunnel. We prayed for her and she was supernaturally healed.

MY FAMILY. My sister and her husband were our most faithful supporters during all our years in Spain. Once they bravely came to Córdoba to visit us in the month of June but the heat was too much for them. After that we usually met up with them on the Costa del Sol where they holidayed each year.

LOST AND FOUND. One occasion stands out in my memory. Imagine an ideal setting. There we were on a beautiful Spanish beach, enjoying the deep blue sea and long stretch of sand, surrounded by a crowd of happy holiday makers. We were meeting up with them and hadn't seen them for some time. Michael, at this time aged about four, was the centre of attention. Each of us kept him happy building sandcastles while we took turns to cool ourselves off by running into the calm but vast Mediterranean sea. I never like to be without a watch on my wrist. Perhaps it's a bit of an obsession with time but on this occasion I had foolishly kept on my mother's gold watch, hardly ideal for a day at the beach. Suddenly I looked at my wrist and exclaimed:

'Help, I've lost my mother's good watch!'

'You mean the gold one' said my sister with a voice full of horror 'with that very expensive bracelet.'

'Yes' I replied with my face bent downwards, not daring to look at her.

'You're not likely to find it here with all these people. Anyhow someone has probably stolen it by now, recognising the value.'

Trying to ignore these negative remarks, of little comfort to me at this crucial moment, I made a quick prayer and continued to dig my hands into the sand around me. As the sand slipped freely beneath my fingers, it had a very calming effect. Inside me I was crying out: *Where God, where do I look?* Less than ten minutes of this activity and I saw something glittering under the sand. There it was, bracelet and all! This time I couldn't contain myself and simply shouted:

'Thank you, God!'

My brother-in-law looked at me in utter disbelief.

'How do you manage it? Things always seem to work out for you!'

'I don't know. Perhaps it's because there is someone up above looking after me, despite all my mistakes.'

11 HOBNOBBING WITH THE FAMOUS

THE RICH & FAMOUS. Pilar, mentioned in chapter nine was the only wealthy lady who ever attended our churches in Spain. She could only come when her husband was away on business or hunting with royalty and such like. It caused quite a stir in the service as she usually arrived in the middle accompanied by her pilot. She would be beautifully dressed with lots of expensive jewellery. The pilot had brought her either in one of their small planes or their large luxurious car. She then greeted the few ladies of her age who had become good friends and was always so excited to be in church. My husband had to get used to the service being interrupted for five minutes or so until she calmed down. I always remember her asking me for tracts that would be suitable to give to the King and Queen whenever they would find themselves in that company. Tracts in those days were so old-fashioned in Spain that I had real difficulty in finding something suitable. She then occasionally wanted to introduce us to some of these famous friends of theirs.

A FAMOUS FILM STAR. One such was Angela Molina, a famous film star. Her father was Antonio Molina, a well-known singer and in fact she comes from a whole family of talented 'artistas' as they say in Spain. Her mother was a friend of Pilar and had been converted later in life. Sadly when she attempted to become part of several churches in Madrid, she ended up being pressurised to give a lot of money and never became part of a local church.

Anyhow, Angela at age 23 was visiting Pilar one day and I got a phone call to see if I could receive them both to visit me. As I prayed I believed God was telling me not to make a fuss or get nervous but just to receive this special lady as I would any more ordinary person. She arrived looking elegant in a beautiful fur coat though it was not particularly cold. Immediately she opened up to me about her life. I had run around my kitchen frantically trying to keep calm and prepare something to offer this lady who was living in France just then making a film with Sophie Loren. However she refused everything I offered as she was suffering from morning sickness and only wanted her chewing gum. She kept giving our four year old more and more chewing gum which kept him happy.

Something odd happened that I can never forget or even explain. A large picture from my wall suddenly fell on her and I was highly embarrassed. However she went on almost oblivious, groaning,

'I feel so wretched, so wretched.'

She wanted my advice about whether she should go to live in her villa in Marbella or the other one in the Canary Islands. I felt quite unprepared to give advice since we didn't then even own one property, never mind having to choose between two or three. When she began to talk about her pregnancy which she didn't want, I felt on safer ground.

I often told my Spanish teenage pupils later about this chat to illustrate that fame and money don't necessarily bring happiness. She told me that she didn't want to marry this guy whose baby she was carrying as she knew she would soon fall in love with someone else. She specialised in nude films. It wasn't at all difficult to talk to her about God and how God could bring peace and satisfaction into her relationships and sex life. Much to my surprise she announced she wanted to attend our church meeting that night which happened to be a prayer meeting.

My husband was out of town preaching elsewhere but as he always jokes that perhaps it was just as well. She was an extremely attractive and sensual lady. Our church members were in a tizzy when they saw who had arrived and she greeted them all with the usual kisses on both cheeks.

No sooner had our meeting begun but she was in floods of tears, declaring out loud

'I want to get right with God. I really need to'.

I did what I could and she prayed a sinner's prayer to receive God into her life but I made one big mistake. I didn't dare ask for her contact details so had no way to follow her up. I was not very bold in those days and much too overawed by the fact that she was famous. Each time I asked Pilar, she was still living in France or

Italy. Later she returned to live in Spain where she is a famous and successful actress as are her children, now adults.

Each visit I made to a hairdresser later when living in Badajoz, I scoured the magazines left there for us to browse through. There was almost sure to be some photo of her or her family and the latest gossip about them. I was relieved to find she did eventually marry and is still with her husband. I have no idea about her relationship now with God and am reminded about the need to follow up folks who become Christians, however difficult that may be.

SPAIN: LAND OF ART AND MUSIC. In Badajoz we met a famous Extremeñan artist and sculptor. Estanislao belonged to the Baptist church there and often complained to us that he had no real friends among the evangelicals in Extremadura as they didn't understand his art. He eventually left the church. Spain seems to be full of artistic and musical people and we must somehow make room for them in our churches.

Wherever we went, we always encouraged folk to write their own songs and music for church. It always seemed out of place to find well known English and German hymns and even choruses being sung in Spanish churches with music that was so inappropriate for the Spanish character. Fortunately that is rarely the case nowadays as the Latin American churches have grown so fast and produced a long list of their own famous songwriters. These songs are now widely sung in all Spanish churches. The more traditional churches still enjoy blasting out 'Onward Christian Soldiers' and similar hymns from time to time, the inheritance left from the many British missionaries who laid down their lives in Spain.

FAITHFUL SERVANTS. I remember meeting one such elderly Brethren missionary and his wife who worked mainly in Galicia and indeed were retired there. I met them just before leaving our comfortable bungalow in Londonderry to go out into the unknown. They were full of stories and seemed such a happy couple, though I noticed they were retired and living in a very basic row of one-storey houses in a remote village in cold and chilly Galicia. I remember praying something like this *Lord, don't let me have such an uncomfortable retirement, please.* Glad to say He answered that prayer. When we returned to live in the UK the climate seemed cold and chilly but after a time it no longer seems so, since we know we are in the right place at the right time.

A MEAL WITH THE ARCHBISHOP. We once had the privilege of being invited to the Catholic archbishop's palace in Badajoz for a meal. That was a really memorable occasion. The night before, we received a phone call from the secretary,

'The archbishop would like you to bring another two Protestant pastors with you' we were told.

We chose our friend Fernando Navarro from the gypsy movement, mentioned in a later chapter and a missionary from Central America.

The vastness of the accommodation and the beauty of the antique furniture all for one single man who lived there left us overawed at first. We were taken from one beautiful reception room to the next and finally into a dining room with expensive heavy dark furniture. At first we were speechless but glad that Fernando was undaunted as usual. He suggested to the archbishop that the priests organise a football match with the Protestant pastors of the town! We laughed heartily and the tension was broken. This particular room was chosen for the meal seemingly because the furniture had been donated by an English family from Jeréz de la Frontera. Several English families had lived there and become famous and rich, with their sherry businesses.

We were shown our seats around this enormous dining table. There were four Catholic priests and four Protestant pastors and I was the only female. I was put at one end of the table and to my horror my husband at the other so it was impossible to speak to one another. The Archbishop sat at the side in the middle and kept ringing a silver bell in front of his plate to call the maid when appropriate. There was so much silver cutlery around my plate that I was slightly confused at one stage. However the priest beside me who was obviously put there to look after me quickly came to my rescue to show me how to use one of the silver utensils to open my walnuts. The food was beautifully presented but rather cold. Dessert was followed by lots of creamy pastry, which most of the priests refused. I was relieved to see that as most of them at the table that day had enormous stomachs protruding well over their trousers bands.

Fortunately when we were given the oranges, I had been taught beforehand how to peel an orange with a knife and fork, never using the fingers. This is part of the protocol when eating with the rich or famous in Spain. The coffee was served in tiny china cups which the Archbishop claimed to be English and appropriate for the occasion. I didn't dare contradict but recognised them as from Limoges, France.

The setting seemed so old-fashioned and unreal that I wanted to giggle but couldn't of course and Desmond was too far away for me to make any comments. We were then taken into the audio-visual room with more valuable pictures. We were so struck by the beauty and modern technology in it all that the Archbishop was quick to point out

'None of these beautiful things belong to me personally; only the books on the bookshelves'.

That then begs the question; *why did the church have to have it all instead of using it to help the poor*?

By this stage of my life I had made several visits to South America where I had seen the extreme poverty in some of the Catholic countries there. The contrast was too much for me that day. That night in bed I had difficulty in sleeping and kept going over the events of the day. I decided that the only thing comparable in my life time was a visit I had made to Windsor Castle.

We did feel the visit was worthwhile since we took along a special version of the Alpha course in France and how it has been accepted by the Catholic hierarchy there. Holy Trinity Brompton church kindly provided this when we wrote to them about our visit. The Archbishop had never heard of Alpha but he and his other priests were very impressed with the presentation. As the archbishop said to us

'We need to learn from you Protestants as you have been so successful in South America'.

MEETING ROYALTY. A chapter on special contacts would be incomplete without a mention of the Duchess of Kent. She was quite well known in Spain as the Honorary President of the Spanish Association against Cancer for many years. On 15 May 1991 during our period of eight years back in the UK (explained in later chapters) we had the honour of meeting her through Desmond's work. She came to open a wing of a hospital for bone marrow transplants. We had to wait a long time before she arrived. The cucumber sandwiches were becoming soggy and we were wilting with the heat under the royal marquee. The atmosphere was electric when she arrived and began walking through the crowd of expectant people. *Who would be chosen for a few minutes conversation with the royal lady?* Desmond whispered:

'We are going to be picked out so prepare yourself. I have prayed and believe God has answered.'

Sure enough we were and even Desmond's boss was ignored on that day much to his annoyance.

After a few minutes conversation with Desmond about the building, she turned to me, looked me straight in the eye and said

'It is just so worthwhile to save lives'.

I was speechless and busy remembering all the protocol we had been warned about through the letter that comes from Buckingham Palace before any royal event. She was referring to the hospital unit that would no doubt save many lives and explaining why she had come instead of being at an important tennis match at Wimbledon that day. For me those words had another meaning and they stuck in my mind for a long time.

We were in the process of deciding whether to return to Spain or take up a very well paid job in Northern England. That would have meant promotion for Desmond. Glad to say in the end Spain won the day and a few years later we heard that the firm had gone bankrupt. God had saved us a lot of heartache and unemployment. His ways are always best.

12 HIGH JINKS IN PALMA

THE BEGINNING OF AN AMAZING CHURCH PLANT. In chapters 9 and 11 I mentioned the wealthy lady Pilar who came from Palma del Río. Its name in English means 'palm tree on the river'. Desmond will start the story of what happened here:

'It was a Sunday morning. The service was ending when the phone rang insistently. Paco, one of the young men in training with us, went to answer it as I finished the service. He came to me afterwards telling me

"Pilar from Palma del Río has rung."

Now, I don't easily claim to hear God's voice speaking to me. It happens on a very rare occasion. This was one of them! I was sure God was telling me to go and visit Pilar that evening. Humanly speaking that was not just unusual but actually quite difficult.

God had been moving in the church over the previous eighteen months and the church was full of new believers, mainly young people but with a sprinkling of older folk. Nobody else had been trained to preach, nor had we left the church alone in that time. What to do with the evening service? However Paco continued speaking and said:

"Pilar wants us to go and visit her this evening".

That was also unusual. Normally she would have come to Córdoba for the service. I took it that God really wanted us to go. I arranged that one of the young men who was most prepared should speak, someone would lead the service and Paco and I went off to visit Pilar. '

When they got to Palma del Río, there was Pilar and another lady. They had an impromptu meeting in Spanish style around the 'brasero'. In those days that was the only form of heating in winter in Spanish homes where we lived. This meant a heater that was either gas, electric or even pieces of burning charcoal under a table that was covered in a thick warm blanket like cloth. It was very cosy to pull this cloth over our knees but did result often in chilblains I found to my cost. This was the focal point in the lounge in winter where folk gathered round to have a chat.

The two ladies pleaded with them to come down to them mid-week for another Bible study. This lady invited her family and Pilar brought her maids. From the very first week folk were getting converted.

Desmond takes up the story once again:

'I had decided to give Félix, one of my young men from Córdoba, a chance to preach and took him with me to Palma del Río. I thought it would be easier for him to give his first message there where the people don't know him. During one of the songs I whispered to him,

"I'll introduce you to speak after this song".

He nodded seriously to me, quite the young preacher ready for his first taste of what it is like. At that point the door opened and in walked three couples in their twenties and a short fat elderly lady. Félix turned white as a sheet and hissed at me:

"I'm not speaking tonight."

I hissed back: "Yes you are".

After a bit of toing and froing it was obvious he was too scared to make his debut there and then. The best laid schemes of mice and men ... The song ended.

Imagine the scene: thirty or forty people packed into a sitting room, all the chairs occupied, the floor covered in bodies, not a space to move. I stood to my feet and started speaking with no preparation. I didn't know where I was going but at the end of a 45-minute message I was aware it was as good an evangelistic message as I had ever wanted to preach. Apparently I prayed for the elderly lady for healing of some physical condition she had but I don't recall the details. All I know was that all seven of those visitors became members of the church. I asked one of them, Modesto, when he and his friends dated their conversion. He looked at me as though I was stupid and replied:

"The first night we came here."

He then went on to tell me how his mother had been healed and the impact this was having in the town. So much was happening so quickly that I often lost track of it all so I stupidly said:

"Oh, how interesting. How did that happen?" Again he looked at me as if I had taken leave of my senses and replied:

"It was you who prayed for her, Ramón."

I nodded sagely and mumbled: "Oh yes, of course."

God was moving in a very special way and we were so happy to see lives changed. All three of those couples later got married and spent some years in full time Christian ministry.'

THE CHURCH IS FORMED. More and more people arrived for the meetings and it became obvious we needed to rent a bigger place. We soon found a house at a cheap price since the owner lived in the Canary Islands and the house was in need of some tender loving care as they say in the UK. In fact the one and only bedroom upstairs had a large gap in the wall. No windows had ever been installed. Nor did it have electricity so in the winter meetings had to be by candlelight. One positive factor was the long winding though rickety stair case which served for the overflow from the meeting held in the downstairs lounge.

By this stage there were so many new Christians to look after that we had to divide our time between Córdoba and Palma del Río. We decided to spend half of our week in one and half in the other. It was quite an effort for me to leave enough food and meals for the young men living with us in our home and prepare food in a cool box to take to Palma where we had no fridge. Then I had to bring all the books and necessary equipment each week to teach our son. He was the one who most enjoyed those weekly stays in the primitive conditions we lived in.

'I really love living here,' he would tell us.

When the new converts heard I was coming to stay, they quickly installed a shower as best they knew how and it was always faulty. They didn't think of cleaning the cement off the tiles and I spent weeks scraping it off. However in that hot and sticky climate I constantly thanked God for their love and for the joy of a cold shower however faulty it may be. My husband felt the people needed to realise that this was their building. They had to learn to provide the furniture, the money for installing the electricity and other necessary amenities so no furniture was brought from our home in Córdoba. We slept on mattresses on the floor as I mentioned in chapter one and used candles by night. We put netting up in the window gaps to protect us from the many insects. It wasn't possible to use electric fans therefore we simply endured the summer heat.

I remember walking into the kitchen and seeing only four bare walls and a sink. My heart sank but it is amazing how cardboard boxes can take the place of cupboards. One small table became a multi-use piece of furniture. We used it not only to eat our meals from but also to prepare all the food and to set the dishes on to drain. I immediately set to and scrubbed the old stone floor on my hands and knees. It reminded me of the floors in the outhouses on my father's farm.

'Never mind', I said to God, 'this is hard but I am happy to obey you.'

As I scrubbed, I suggested that Desmond search the house thoroughly for any traces of rats or mice as the house had been empty and closed up for many years. He assured me he had found no traces of those delightful animals and I was relieved. Glad to say we only continued this routine for about six months. During that time the people learnt to tithe (freely give one tenth of their income) and as well as that give generously to the work of the church.

BEING A CURIOSITY IN A SMALL TOWN. In a small town like Palma del Río anything non-Catholic is looked on with great suspicion. As I joined the neighbours at the corner of the road each evening with my new sparkling tin jug awaiting the milk lady's arrival, I was somewhat of a curiosity for all. We never knew exactly when she would arrive on her motor bike with a large tin can of fresh milk on each side of it and her enormous ladle. If I arrived too late there was no milk. If I arrived too early questions were fired at me such as the usual

'You Protestants don't believe in the virgin, do you?'

One day someone remarked that I must have a very wealthy and generous father with a large estate that we could live in Spain without working! I was so fed up with all the questions by this stage that I simply answered:

'Yes, I do'.

I quickly went back inside and thanked God, my Father for all his generosity to us. He was indeed a wealthy Father. I did appreciate the fresh milk which we then boiled and it always had lots of cream on top but I didn't appreciate all the questions that went with it. Of course I was young and still very concerned about what others thought about me. I'm glad to say after the years of service abroad you learn to be more concerned with what God thinks of you and less and less about others' opinions. We will always stand out from the crowd.

PETRA, A CHARACTER WE CAME ACROSS. One lady comes to mind. When we first met Petra she uttered a mouthful of words we didn't understand. Later it was explained to us that she was the most foul-mouthed woman of the town so we wouldn't want to learn those words. She had five children and worked in the local fruit factory as well as selling clothes from door to door. She was not beyond selling her body either. It was not difficult to talk to her about the Lord as she began to open up to us about her life of suffering. She also claimed that God had told her He was not interested in forms and rituals but in communication with man on a personal basis. A tract had been put in her letter box one day (later we discovered it was by some Germans on holiday in Spain connected to our mission). When she read it, she knew at once in her spirit that this was truth and searched high and low for the folk who had distributed that tract.

Petra started to attend our meetings and realised this was the truth she was searching for. It was such a joy to see her clean up her life and talk to many about her new-found faith. We used to think of her as our Mary Magdalene. I still remember my first visit to her flat. The scene was quite chaotic. Her elderly father lived with her and her children were a law unto themselves. To me they seemed like little street urchins. The standard of hygiene left much to be desired and I sometimes despaired of them. Obviously God didn't, for they were some of the first Spanish children we saw responding to the Holy Spirit. All five of them ranging from six to twelve years of age were filled with the Holy Spirit in our meetings. On one occasion I spent the night with her eldest son in hospital as he was delirious with typhoid.

FIRST BAPTISMS IN PALMA DEL RÍO

Eventually a charitable organisation did pay for all the children to be educated in a very strict and rather poor type of boarding school. She meanwhile had bought a small plot in the country and started to build with her own hands a very crude dwelling. She even went to classes to learn how to install the electricity! a real character indeed.

OUR FIRST BAPTISMS IN THE TOWN. Our first baptisms were arranged at a nearby lake. Our Córdoba church had a baptismal tank, suitable for adult baptisms but we wanted to be near the village to allow family and friends to be invited. It was a day of great celebration when thirty people from Palma del Río were baptised. We invited Daniel del Vecchio to join us in baptising the new converts. He was the most successful foreign missionary in Spain at that time and we wanted to learn from him. We had visited his church in Torremolinos and his communities (mainly made up of converted drug addicts) in Málaga. This was where his pastors were being trained.

RELATIONSHIPS WITH OTHER PASTORS. For some years we did enjoy a relationship with this unique American missionary. All through our lives we have believed in spending time with other servants of God who are more successful and more experienced than we are. We visited his Spanish churches and even had some of his pastors in training to preach in our church in Córdoba from time to time.

One had a very powerful testimony. He stayed for a few days in our home and I will never forget the details of that testimony for he had been a homosexual and with God's help was able to change his sexual orientation. It is not politically correct in some circles to admit that homosexuals can successfully make such changes but there was the evidence before my eyes. Later I met a lesbian who had a similar testimony. When we were at a pinnacle of success shall we say in our new-found ministry in Spain, we attracted Daniel's attention and he invited us to join up with him. However as we prayed about it, God did not give us any confirmation. Without that we couldn't leave our German link which we had then and our team of three couples, the German, the Spanish and ourselves.

We were three strong couples, each from very different cultures and each with our own distinct ideas about church. There were sometimes heated arguments among us all and once two German pastors came to sort us out. On another occasion two YWAM leaders had to come from Madrid to do the same. In those visits we learned a lot about how to 'live peaceably with all men' (Romans 12:18). Today we count those two couples among our best friends and can laugh about our difficulties of the past. We certainly didn't then.

Team relationships on the mission field are an area where the enemy attacks with forceful opportunism. He recognises that unity in the team is vital to the progress of the Gospel and that healthy and meaningful relationships are key to wellbeing and productivity. Therefore, he seeks to disrupt, cause misunderstandings and create rifts between people. Having left good relationships behind to follow the call of God, establishing new, realistic and enduring relationships is so important. If these relationships go sour, the pain is very intense. Some missions have turned to DISC consultants/facilitators to help teams relate in a productive, valuing and honouring manner. For help in these matters we recommend Jan Whitmore and Mintie Nel (www.makingdisciples.co.uk) Both have been missionaries themselves and pastors to missionaries for more than 25 years. Jan is an accredited facilitator of Sharpening Your People Skills (SYPS), often known as DISC. This tool aids productivity and relational effectiveness in the workplace. Firstly, it helps leaders and followers recognise and acknowledge strengths and weaknesses in their mission team. Then, it teaches relationship versatility-how team members can champion one person's strength to cover another's weakness. Thus, the team operates in strength and become encouragers one of the other. For more than 30 years, DISC has helped people deal more effectively with conflict and value the contribution of differences. Another helpful website is www.walkthru.org/trainthetrainer.

HANDING ON THE BATON. With travelling back and forth from Córdoba we soon saw the need to give the work over to another pastor and one of Daniel's Spanish pastors seemed the obvious choice. He, with the practical help of the church members, knocked down that old house and built a super American like church building on the same spot. It was one of the first 'church like' buildings in that part of Spain. Three of the young couples later went into full time work.

Desmond had the pleasure of speaking in that church in September 2013. It is now pastored by a Spaniard who graduated from the Assemblies of God Bible College in Córdoba (working very closely with our Córdoba church). The church is part of the Baptist Union in Spain and our friends in Córdoba felt strongly that Desmond should visit the church when passing through that region so it was quickly arranged in true Spanish style. You can imagine his delight to see many of our original converts at that meeting nearly 40 years later. In fact, one, Modesto, who had long ago left the church heard that Desmond was coming to preach and came especially because of that. This does not make us proud but humble as we know that anything we achieved in ministry in Spain was only by the grace of God. It does remind us of a truth we already know that the Spaniards do not forget easily their 'spiritual Fathers in the Lord'. There is always a special bond that is not easily broken even though the next pastor may be excellent. Since then Modesto has seemingly never looked back.

13 RUNNING ON EMPTY

A TIME OF PAIN. By 1983 the church had grown to about sixty, a good number for a Spanish evangelical church at that time. Leaders had been trained and lots of young men and women discipled by my husband and myself. The young men living with us were travelling to evangelise in some nearby towns such as Montilla and Cabra. The presence of God was very strong in the meetings and many were having dreams and visions and exercising the gifts of the Spirit as in 1 Cor. 12, 13 and 14. What we were not prepared for was the envy that suddenly appeared among some of them.

Strangely enough it involved me as a woman in ministry. Several told Desmond that they thought I was taking too much part in the public meetings. I was prophesying and leading worship. I had begun by playing the old organ, later an old piano and then my good Lowden guitar. However in every church we moved to in Spain, we had the same story. I began leading the worship and playing the only instrument. Not being the best of musicians, I always prayed for more musicians to be converted and even taught them a little of guitar to gain their interest. Sure enough each time the musicians have soon been converted.

The crunch came when Desmond asked me to preach one evening and this I did although somewhat nervous. I was even more nervous when before my eyes six of our young disciples got up and walked out after about five minutes of my carefully prepared sermon. One of these was a young girl I had spent a lot of time with as I recognised her gift with children. Her family could not have afforded to pay for further education so I trained her as a Sunday school teacher, then trained her to teach Spanish reading to our son. Finally when we set up a small pre-school in the church building (more of that in chapter 25) she was the assistant teacher along with myself. I simply couldn't believe it. We later received a message from them that what I was doing was unbiblical and they could not return to be part of our church.

There followed a church members' meeting where voices were raised. In fact there was so much shouting that our son, trying to sleep upstairs was disturbed and remarked later

'How could those people shout at my Daddy?'

They moved to be part of another church in the town but very soon left that to begin their own church. They desperately wanted more leadership opportunities. All sorts of rumours were spread around about me and Desmond and I were heartbroken. We went through a lot of soul searching in those days and poured out our hearts before God. There were many tears and a well-known pastor came especially from Madrid to try to bring about reconciliation but was unsuccessful. Even a gypsy pastor came. I still remember that pastor crying openly and saying

'I cannot bear to see my dear sister treated like this'.

You see he had become a good friend since I was teaching his son at that time along with our own son (also more about that in chapter 24). The church was left wounded and since we were too, it was difficult to help them. I myself did not want to do anything publicly in church services for a very long time until God healed me of all that attack on me as a woman in ministry. Even today I am quick to jump to the defence of any lady who is suffering simply because she has a calling and is trying to carry it out. I cannot bear to let anyone suffer all that cruel spiritual abuse. The truth of Galatians 3:28 became very real to me in those days. 'There is neither male nor female; for you are all one in Christ Jesus'.

We realised we needed some time out. It was arranged that Ignacio would look after the church while we returned to the UK for a sabbatical. We were thoroughly burnt out.

NO RESIDENCE PERMITS FOR MISSIONARIES. When we first arrived in Córdoba, no Protestant missionaries were getting residence permits. The only way to stay in Spain was to leave every six months and have our passports stamped. We could have used that time to have a short break but we usually went to Morocco and came back as quickly as possible. If the spiritual atmosphere was heavy in Spain, it was even heavier in Morocco.

Our young son noticed that and often cried, saying,

'I want to go back home'.

The Moroccans met us at the boat, taking pictures without permission which we later were almost forced to pay for before leaving. They used every opportunity to get money from us, putting our son up on a camel's back which demanded another photo of course. A snake charmer then curled a snake around his neck and we were ourselves ready for home. We always thanked God for Catholic Spain. It did not have that terrible poverty we encountered in Morocco and where the anger and greed in people's eyes were so clearly to be seen.

BACK IN NORTHERN IRELAND. With a very heavy heart, we left the church and spent our sabbatical year in Northern Ireland. We had found a place to stay in a Christian community where Michael had suitable friends of his age but soon we realised it was really going off beam and we got out. Instead we lived with Desmond's father and took over the running of his home as well as going back to home-schooling so it wasn't really the relaxation we had hoped for.

14 THE DRUG REHABILITATION CENTRE

IN CÓRDOBA ONCE MORE. When we got back to Spain, we had to face the situation again of a wounded and much depleted church. Rather than go back to live in the same place, we decided to live in a flat kindly rented to us by a couple in the church. This meant a clearer separation between church and home. We no longer had to cope with the many visitors each evening to the building. They would come for music practice, drama practice, making visual aids for Sunday service or simply to see one another. A strong sense of family was always instilled in our churches wherever we went. The move proved to be a big help to us both. Now we were able to spend more time alone as a family which is so vital for any pastor. We had not completely forgotten our vision to reach out to the needy and the addicts but we realised that that required other premises. Eventually we saw our vision fulfilled but not in the way we had imagined it.

NEW HOPE, NEW PARTNERS. A new missionary had come into the area called Mario Fumero, originally from Cuba but with many years in Honduras where he had set up several successful drug rehabilitation centres. In fact he was so well thought of there that the government later lent him their military helicopters to organise evacuation work when Honduras was severely flooded. Some folk who had been visiting our church such as the family of Esteban Muñoz, began to meet with Mario. They accepted his vision to set up a drug rehabilitation centre.

Esteban was only 14 when he first arrived at our church and little did we realise that he was to become the future pastor of the work. As we got to know Mario and his Norwegian wife, we realised they would be the ideal couple for us to join up with so we did. We provided the church building, the government recognition for a church and some older well-established Christians. They provided all the experience in working with drug addicts, which we didn't have.

MOVING TO THE DRUG REHABILITATION CENTRE. By this time Mario had already bought some land outside the city in a mountainous area where the addicts would be well cut off from any temptations connected with a large city. He suggested that Desmond begin to prepare the site for sowing fruit and vegetables, which he did along with our young folk. Mario would be the official pastor of the two groups that had joined together and we were happy and indeed relieved at that arrangement.

In June 1984 it was decided that we should go to live at the centre to prepare for the intake of the first drug addicts. The house on the site was very small. However, I was given the bait of designing and planting flowers in a large rockery in front of it and that satisfied me at first. I felt under a lot of pressure with our living conditions. In fact the bedroom was not big enough to hold both a wardrobe and bed and Desmond's solution was simply to shorten the bed by cutting off its end! Even with that we could not both dress or undress together. There simply was no space for that. I didn't let Desmond forget that for some time and now we can simply laugh about it when we do marriage counselling. I certainly didn't laugh then.

The kitchen was even worse and neither our washing machine nor fridge would fit in. This time the solution was to extend the kitchen so we got a cement mixer which I somehow learnt to operate. It was quite a case of necessity. No one today can believe that is possible but I do have the photos to prove it. Then our washing machine broke down and the technician who came refused to fix it. According to him, it was in an impossible situation stuck in there as it was in a very small space of our 'newly extended' kitchen. That seemed to be the last straw and I remember being in such floods of tears that Desmond decided to try to fix the washing machine himself. Much to his surprise and my frantic prayers, the machine was working again.

OUR FIRST ARRIVALS. The first drug addicts to arrive were a father and son. The son was only 12 and since our son was nine, they became friends. He kept asking Michael questions like

'Have you never hit your teacher? Have you never smoked dope?'

Michael would repeat all these conversations to us. Since smoking of any sort was forbidden at the centre, he would show Michael these wild plants around the hillside which according to him might be suitable for making drugs. Another early addict we had was an 18 year old boy, son of a college lecturer, whose brain was badly affected by the use of drugs. This was hardly the ideal situation in which to bring up a nine-year-old boy. There was so much work to be done after the move that we had to leave the home-schooling for a month. Michael was helping his father instead with all the practical work that had to be done on the farm. For me he had to read the then famous book *The Cross and the Switchblade* by David Wilkerson. That would give him all the information he needed to know about drugs and then at mealtimes, we discussed the book together.

I realised I was becoming very tense and fearful again and was looking forward to another trip to Northern Ireland that May of 1984. Years later I can look back and realise that in fact this time was not encouraging our son Michael to experiment with drugs but doing the opposite. It was educating him at an early age about the terrible consequences of taking any sort of drugs. It was no surprise that one of his first areas of Christian service when he began as a pilot in Manchester was to become a volunteer in a Christian drug rehabilitation centre there.

AN AMAZING JOURNEY. I should mention at this stage a wonderful experience we had some years earlier on a journey back to the UK. Our car broke down in the middle of France and hours were spent in a garage having it repaired. By this time, we were seriously doubting whether we would get to Calais in time for the boat across the channel. It was already dark and difficult to see cheap hotels or guest houses to stay the night. Several had refused us, saying they were full up. In desperation we stopped and asked at a garage if they knew of somewhere. They pointed us in the direction of a large house in its own grounds.

'We don't exactly know what sort of a place it is but we do see a lot of groups of people coming and going from there so you could try' they said.

When we got to the gate, we were surprised to see the name of a Bible college that we had already heard of. In fact in our Bible College in Denmark a lecturer from there had come to teach us for a week. He was actually Welsh so, since we were the only British students there, he had taken a special interest in us. He had asked to receive our prayer letters once we got to Spain. We saw that the gate was locked and a notice saying they were closed for the holiday period. However we remembered the name of the lecturer and rang the bell asking to speak to him. Imagine our delight when he welcomed us with open arms, saying

'This is amazing. I have just been reading your recent prayer letter and praying for you'.

Moreover he had planned to be away at a conference on those dates but then believed he should be resting instead. He was a gentleman in his mid eighties.

We were immediately taken in to the college, given a super French meal, which is perhaps my favourite type of food and the most comfortable beds you could imagine. That included our friend Stanley who had been visiting us and was travelling back with us. We slept like logs and got up refreshed and ready to set off early next morning. After driving all day, we arrived at the boat just in time. The whole experience was such a reminder of God's care for us. There are so few Bible Colleges in France and who would have thought that we would simply come on one of them without any previous planning. God's ways are amazing.

ANOTHER MIRACULOUS EXPERIENCE. Perhaps it is just as well that that incident was still pretty fresh in my memory. Desmond suddenly announced to me before another journey to Northern Ireland that there was no money for supplies on our journey. He suggested I take tins out of my cupboard and also our gas cooker so that we could cook on the way. We had a small tent to stay in as we drove up through Spain and France. Some YWAM friends in Madrid had invited us to stay for the first night. I'm glad to say they were extremely generous and gave us quite a lot of food for the next day! After that it was cooking all sorts of strange meals from the tins. We arrived at the channel crossing late at night.

Desmond suggested we sleep a little in the queue of cars and wait for the ferry at four am as the fare then was cheaper.

In those days there were no travel agencies in Córdoba to buy our boat tickets from so we usually bought them at the harbour office just before boarding. What Desmond didn't tell me was that he hadn't got enough money for the fares even at the cheaper rate. While Michael and I slept, he spent most of the hours talking to God. He counted over his French francs again and again, just to check there was no mistake. *Perhaps there was another note there that he had missed! Perhaps he had mistaken the price of the tickets* but no! The price was clearly written at the dock where we were waiting.

As he approached the counter to buy the tickets, he said he was absolutely numb. Here he was with a family in a car to get to Northern Ireland. He had used the rest of his money to fill up the petrol tank which would get us to England and no further. If God didn't turn up now, we were in serious trouble. He took out the French franc notes again to give them to the ticket officer. This time as he counted the notes, to his amazement, there was an extra one! We got our tickets and sailed to the UK. To this day, Desmond claims it was supernatural like the multiplying of the loaves and fishes.

THE FINAL LAP OF THE JOURNEY TO NORTHERN IRELAND. We were due to stay with Alwyn and Mary Harland. Desmond had met Alwyn when he was a child at the Children's Special Service Mission (CSSM), part of Scripture Union, and Alwyn was the leader. Later Desmond was to join his team of leaders and he visited us several times in Spain. Alwyn always had had a big influence on his life and we knew we had to listen, when he questioned us about returning to ministry in Spain. He remarked that I seemed to be extremely stressed but little did he know of course about our difficult journey up until that point. He suggested it might be time for a change of direction, which was very hard for Desmond to hear but he received it.

Another surprise came our way. We were invited to speak to Alwyn's congregation that Sunday morning about our work in Spain. The pastor was Iain Kirby, another friend from the past. We were given a generous offering which meant we had the money now for the petrol and ferry across to Northern Ireland. 'Hairy' experiences like these certainly keep you close to God! When we finally arrived at my parents' home, there was a letter from one of our supporters with an unexpected cheque for £1,000 (a substantial amount of money in 1984).

THE CÓRDOBA CHURCH TODAY. We had left the Córdoba church without even a farewell but it was good to be able to visit it many times later and see what had come from those humble beginnings. The church has now over 300 members and has planted out 13 new churches in the region. The drug rehabilitation centre that we helped start is well recognised by the local authorities who often send cases to it. In fact they were so impressed that they asked them to set up a centre for juvenile delinquents on the same site. The church has its own psychologists, social workers, doctors and other professionals. In our time there weren't any of those but those we ministered to went on to work hard and study. The church that was very much working class when we pastored it, has now become largely middle class and is very active in society. The prison work continues and the church has set up a centre for battered wives. They together with the other churches also have a ministry to prostitutes and a hospital and residential care home visitation programme. The pastor Esteban is a very well known figure as vice president of the Assemblies of God in Spain. From small beginnings great things grow! Our visits there always give us a lot of joy and we are still well received and respected.

15 WHEN ENOUGH IS ENOUGH

TIME TO RETURN, RECOVER AND REBUILD.

'We think it's time for you to come home.'

To my husband these words sounded like a death knell to our vision of serving God in Spain. To me they sounded a blessed relief from the pressures we had been living under. The four men in Northern Ireland who had acted as trustees for our work told us they had all come to that conclusion. You can be so immersed in a situation that you don't see the bigger picture. In the eight years we had been in Spain we had come to an end of our resources and become isolated from our support base. It was time to RETURN, RECOVER and REBUILD. One of these offered us the use of his large caravan at Groomsport, Co. Down which we gladly accepted until we could make more permanent arrangements for our future.

When we told our son, by now ten years old that we were not going back to live in Spain, he burst into tears. That for him was home and he had his friends there. Glad to say the church we joined made sure he soon had plenty of friends of his age.

We began to attend Kings Fellowship in Bangor led by John and Barbara Kelly whom we had known through university and CSSM. It was then a large fellowship meeting in the Methodist church and was in the process of becoming a church. The building they bought was just across the road from the sea. As we watched the waves splashing, it was therapeutic during this time of change which we hadn't planned for. The care we received from the members of that fellowship was unbelievable and we were pleased to be close to our families again.

BUILDING UP A HOME ONCE MORE. It was arranged that only Desmond would return to Spain with a car and trailer to collect our essential items. There was no finance to bring over more. Meanwhile Michael and I were to live for a month with a widow called Jenny and her daughter. Never did we imagine that Jenny would later marry John Kelly after he lost his wife. Jenny than rented us her previous house before we were able to get a mortgage and buy our own home again. The church members heard of furniture that was going free and soon we had a house full of furniture once more. In fact one of the leaders had made a list with me of what was needed for every room. We prayed and she spread the word around. It was amazing to see how little by little everything was ticked off that list.

ANOTHER MOVE TO ENGLAND. After a short period employed by an audiovisual firm, the church suggested a new job for Desmond. He was to set up his own business along with a converted former Catholic priest who now had a wife and two small children. A year later we realised that the business was not providing enough for two families so we decided it was best to leave it with the ex-priest and we moved to England. This came about through the visit of a pastor to Kings Fellowship from a group of churches that had had grown out of the house church movement in England in the seventies. He suggested that Desmond go over to Basingstoke, Hampshire for a week.

'Let's just see if any job is available'.

Immediately he got a job. I was distraught at having to leave my family after two good years of being closer to them. The one thing that attracted me was the offer of teaching modern languages in the Christian school there.

With a heavy heart we moved again. This time Desmond was recovering from a bout of pneumonia so I had to do most of the packing myself with the help of the church members. We had just finished decorating our new home and Michael was happily settled in a prestigious grammar school in Bangor so it was not easy to leave all that behind. Moreover I was giving up a very enjoyable job as Spanish assistant in that school as well as evening work in adult education, teaching my three foreign languages. Since we were moving to rented accommodation which was furnished, we had to leave our furniture in the attic at my parents' house.

The first few weeks to my horror were spent in a caravan. It was not the beautiful caravan site at Groomsport, Northern Ireland, but a caravan in a very damp farmer's field in southern England. I struggled to adjust to yet more changes and I remember making a list of all the advantages of living in England, all the things I had to be thankful for. Each morning I read this aloud to myself to re-train and renew my mind. I didn't understand in those days that those who flow with change rather than resist it are less stressed, healthier and generally happier. To walk with God and fulfil His will, we need to have a mindset that adapts to change however costly and uncomfortable it may be.

DEATH OF BOTH PARENTS. In May 1987 my father died followed two years later by my mother. I was very grateful to be in the UK for their funerals. It was good to be able to see my father before he died but my mother died so suddenly that I only arrived in time for her funeral. At first there was no time for grief, as I had to help my sister quickly clear out my parents' bungalow. However, when I got back to Basingstoke during a prayer meeting, the tears began to flow and I wondered when they would ever stop. I realised I was carrying grief not only for my mother's death but for the sad events that had happened in Spain and then our sudden parting from Northern Ireland and the family once again. It was very much a healing time of my emotions.

TEACHING IN A SCHOOL AGAIN AND BEYOND. Two Australians were to become influential in our lives - Ron and Sue Trudinger. Ron had been a pioneer missionary teacher with the Aborigines and had translated the Bible into their language. He was still a missionary at heart and quickly told us

'I think you will be back in Spain again'.

This comment did not bless me at the time. We had just bought a house, thanks to the legacy from my parents' will and two kind church members who lent us money to help us get a mortgage. I am very much a home-maker and couldn't bear thinking of leaving yet another home that I had put my own stamp on. As Ron had prophesied we spent only five years in that home before returning to Spain. The call on our lives to Spain was still there and could not be forgotten.

Meanwhile, I found myself as Head of Modern Languages in a Christian School founded by Ron but with few resources. My first Spanish lessons were given in a cold dark Second World War bunker. However, my experience in Spain gave me faith to believe God and bring Him into all my decisions. I was no longer a professional depending on my own mind but very much depending on the Holy Spirit. Twice I was head-hunted by the local sixth form college and offered a very attractive job teaching A-Level Spanish there but I immediately refused despite the good salary promised. My love for languages seemed to be contagious and it was very satisfying to see a considerable number of my pupils go on to study languages at degree level. What was even more exciting was to be able to instil in the pupils a love for mission and some went abroad later to serve God. These were not only the ones who had a gift for languages but also those who had struggled.

Occasionally I brought some needy Spaniards into my classes and the pupils had prepared songs and choruses to sing to them and had even made paella! The Spaniards, far from their own family and country ended up usually in tears. The Holy Spirit was touching them without them realising what was happening. We organised one of my classes to visit Córdoba in May 1991 and stay with teenagers from several of the churches in the city. As we were later to do in Badajoz, we helped with English classes in two different schools and at lunch time put on a pre-evangelistic performance. This was a great success.

I began to attend and take part in conferences of the Christian Schools Trust. Since I was one of the oldest and more experienced language teachers, I was given the job of organising and speaking at the seminars. This led on to a weekend training conference for them at Stapleford Centre, near Nottingham. It was then the centre for the Association of Christian Teachers (ACT). I became co-editor of a magazine for Christian language teachers as well as leading a working party of foreign language teachers from Christian Schools. This group then joined together with a group of similar teachers in the state system. Out of this merge came the CHARIS project; a unique series of textbooks promoting moral and spiritual development through the Modern Languages Curriculum.

It was a very fulfilling time for me in those years and a time of restoration. Psalm 71: 20-21 became a reality. 'Though you have made me see troubles, many and bitter, you will restore my life

MISSION TRIP TO CORDOBA

again, from the depths of the earth, you will again bring me up. You will increase my honour and comfort me once again.' I began to understand myself more and tried to deal with my perfectionist tendencies, my desire to control my situation, or rather tried to let God deal with these tendencies that were very deep within me since childhood.

MISSION TRIPS TO CÓRDOBA. Desmond was able to organise two mission trips back to Córdoba. A group of English church members attempted to build a multi-purpose hall on the drug rehabilitation centre we had left. The next one was to build a gym. Few people on the team had any building experience so it was a big challenge as well as the high summer temperatures of 45 degrees. The church in England was very middle class and in Córdoba they found themselves camping on the same site as drug addicts being rehabilitated. One 55 year old Secondary School headmaster was deeply affected by the trip. Peter Sayer and his wife decided to leave their careers after the moving experience and dedicate themselves to missionary service. Others claimed that their lives changed after the trip.

16 ONCE MORE INTO THE BREACH

THE BIG DECISION. Finally, it was decided. After lots of consultation, in 1993, we were going back to Spain, back to God's calling for our lives. We had recovered, rebuilt and now we were returning to the fray. After successful A-Levels our son was given a grant from the Ministry of Defence. He had to spend a year working for them in Malvern before going to university and then they would sponsor him throughout his university career. That was such a blessing for us and freed us economically to consider going back to Spain.

By this time my husband was doing well in his job selling prefabricated buildings. He had studied to get a diploma in marketing. In fact, he was offered a job as national sales and marketing manager based at their Northern office. There is often an attractive alternative when we want to find God's path for our life. Though it sounded so good we knew our destiny still lay in Spain so he refused the offer. In fact some years later, we heard that the firm had gone bankrupt so we realised how God had protected us once more and was clearly leading us.

All three of us talked together about the decision of going back to Spain and Michael encouraged us to go, assuring us that he knew we were made for Spain. Our pastor at that time also talked to him to make sure that he was in a fit place to manage without his parents close by. He was well aware of some missionaries' children who had become resentful and felt rejected by their parents' zeal for God's work in another nation.

NEW CONNECTIONS WITH BADAJOZ. We had been uncertain about where to return to in Spain. Should we return to Córdoba or go to Seville where our German friends (the pastors who had welcomed us in Córdoba) were now working as part of YWAM? Another possibility had now opened to us. There was a Spanish lady and close friend in our church called Piedy Palmer whose 14-year-old niece came to visit her from Badajoz in Extremadura. I was looking after her when she attended the

Christian school where I taught and made sure she heard the gospel message.

She happened to be accompanying her aunt in a planning meeting for one of the building trips to Córdoba. Suddenly this girl burst into tears. She assured us they were tears of joy. Desmond's Spanish Bible was on the table and she had seen a great light come from the Bible that almost blinded her eyes. She exclaimed

'At last I've found what I was looking for!'

She had sought in the Catholic church and had been afraid to even pass by the one Protestant church in her native city. She had been warned against it. Now she was experiencing the living God and went back to tell her family and friends. Six months later we went to visit Estela and her mother Maruja with another couple, Edwin and Margaret Monger. This couple was to have a big influence for many years in our life and were especially caring to us.

Maruja was very concerned about her daughter refusing to go back to the Catholic church with her since her trip to England. We suggested they both come with us to visit a Pentecostal church we had heard about in Badajoz. Maruja was then converted and both she and her daughter remained in that church for some years. When she was baptised, the pastor invited Desmond to join him in the ceremony and Estela came back to England to be baptised. She had become good friends with our son and his group of teenage friends.

Now there were three possibilities: to return to Córdoba, Seville or Badajoz? Desmond made an exploratory trip with another English pastor to those three places and Badajoz was the clear winner. We received prophecies to confirm it and remembered how many years before when living in Córdoba, we actually thought of going west to Extremadura. That was the poorest and most primitive part of Spain. In fact, Desmond had received this in prayer about going as far as Badajoz and then into Portugal and we had almost forgotten it.

We decided to take a group of English young folk out to Badajoz to work with that Pentecostal church. That was a very fruitful time. The pastor had arranged for us to go into a local school to give

English lessons and I made friends with the teacher. We had open air meetings in a park and several young people were converted. One was Paco, who later was the first person we baptised when we went to live there. That visit made us more and more sure that we were meant to go to live in that city.

ANOTHER POSSIBILITY. Bob and Vicky Lichty met up with us in London during our eight year period back in the UK mainly because of their interest in Michael's education. They were particularly interested in his integration into the British education system, since they had been the ones advising us to home-school him. They were at that time based in Hawaii at the University of the Nations. Their proposal later was to return to Spain and set up a base in Extremadura.

'You Desmond can continue with your gifting in church planting and Caroline can be involved in educational projects with us,' they suggested.

It was a very attractive proposal. Our relationship had been tried and tested and come out the other side. However, we knew that our priority was always church planting and that has never been the main thrust of YWAM. We didn't want to be diverted. We returned to Badajoz to plant another church. In fact, God never allowed Bob and Vicky to return to live in Spain, though they did meet up with us in some of their visits back to the country.

One significant visit was in 2009. We had just gone through a very dramatic and painful change in our ministry. Bob and Vicky were now considered to be one of the apostolic figures in YWAM, since they founded the YWAM bases in the country. However, when they heard indirectly of our circumstances, they immediately changed their plans. We were privileged to receive a visit instead of the other YWAM bases. It was a very important time of healing for both of us.

SAD FAREWELLS. In January 1993 we made a wise decision to rent out our home and someone from the church promised to look after it for us. I still remember the last weekend Michael spent in our home before we left. We had our friends Alwyn and Marie Harland to stay as well, which fortunately took our minds off the sad parting with our son. The only consolation for me was to think of how God must have felt when he gave up his son to go to the cross. That helped me a little keep in perspective what to me seemed a very big sacrifice.

The church had a lovely farewell service for us with a special cake decorated in icing with Spanish fans and the words in Spanish of the Aaronic blessing (Numbers 6:24-26). Wherever I go, I still have a picture of that beautiful cake in my lounge for all to see and admire. It was particularly moving for me when a pastor's wife stood up and gave me a prophetic word. You see I was struggling to leave all my new found friends in England, friends who shared with me their interest in Christian Education. The word was

'You will have a special friend there in Badajoz, maybe even in the block of flats where you will be living'.

Just at the last minute my husband had a bad flu and tonsillitis. This meant that once again I was responsible for our packing. We had hired a large lorry which was to be driven by some unemployed men from our church, with us following in our little English Ford Fiesta. This time we were having an electrician with us to check out the electrics of our flat, which to me was a great luxury. This time I could take a good cooker with us, which he would connect for us. I didn't have to put up with Spanish ones that couldn't be regulated easily for baking though now they can. I didn't have to go back to the memories of that old church house in Córdoba where often as I put in a plug, dangerous looking sparks came out or I got an electric shock.

Edwin Monger felt strongly that we as missionaries should have an equivalent salary to the pastors from our church and talked to our church elders about that. They instead believed we should go as bi-vocational missionaries this time. Desmond was given an offer by the Christian firm where he had worked before when we first arrived in England. He was to sell business partnering plans to businesses in Spain on a commission basis and the church was to send us a small amount each month. We were given a special offering to help with the expense of the move. The church had done everything to make the transition as easy as possible.

We left very early in the morning to catch the ferry but that didn't stop one family coming with their four children (the Asprays) to wave at us from the bridge over the motorway. The children were holding up a large 'God bless you' sign that they had made in Spanish. That was a gesture that we really appreciated. It was symbolic that this time we were going to be cared for by a church that was behind us. We had always regretted the previous experience from Londonderry. The church we had left had a big division a few years after we left for Spain. On returning, we visited the two groups but felt misunderstood by the other side because we did just that. It is so important for missionaries to know and feel they are cared for by the church back at home.

The journey back to Spain was not easy as Desmond was so unwell. In fact, it was just when we were in the middle of the Bay of Biscay that he said he suddenly regained strength. We wondered if the enemy had not been trying to prevent our return to the country of our destiny. However half way there, he must have realised it was a lost cause and Desmond regained his health. At that point in the journey the ship's engines stopped and we were floating aimlessly for some time. We hardly noticed it ourselves but other passengers were very frightened. We had a lot of mixed emotions about going back and so much to talk about. It was not like the first time when you embark on a completely new venture with God. This time there was no excitement of the unknown. We knew only too well the battles that surely lay ahead.

OUR CHURCH SENDS US OFF WITH A BEAUTIFUL CAKE

FIVE AM. ON A MOTORWAY BRIDGE

17 A NEW ADVENTURE - EXTREMADURA

EARLY DAYS IN THE NEW CITY. What a sensation! The narrow and busy side road next to our flat was closed to traffic to let us unload. Tongues were wagging. *Who on earth was arriving from England to sleepy Badajoz?* We were very grateful not to be going back on our own. A younger couple we had known from Kings Fellowship, Bangor had agreed to come with us. Their commitment was for four years. Anthony and Susan Johnston with their daughter Hanna were waiting for us when we arrived as well as Zoe, a former Spanish pupil of mine and her husband Matt. Zoe had already arrived in October to spend an academic year in Badajoz as part of her university course.

It was so good to have all their help as we took our furniture out of the lorry and up to the third floor of a large apartment building in Santa Maria de la Cabeza Square, Badajoz. I was hoping that as we had both lost our bright auburn coloured hair, we would not stand out so easily as foreigners. In fact, we still did. As before we attracted many comments in English from young teenagers as we walked along the street, such as

'Good morning, how are you?'

I was often told that even my way of walking was English though I fail to see how. We had made every effort we could to adapt to the culture.

Desmond had made a trip beforehand to Badajoz and thanks to Maruja (mentioned in the last chapter), he had found this spacious flat to rent. We were so conscious that we had found through Maruja that worthy house mentioned in Matthew 10:11-13 and she was to become a very significant lady in our time in Badajoz. I hadn't seen the flat but I realised that God understood my sense of colour. When I walked in and saw the lovely marble floor, I cried out

'Thank you God.'

Even our three-piece-suite matched perfectly!

ANTHONY & SUSAN JOHNSTON, OUR FIRST CO-WORKERS

OUR FIRST IMPRESSIONS. Badajoz in Extremadura was a city of some 150,000 inhabitants. Its strategic position on the Portuguese border, midway between Lisbon and Madrid, on the important main route that unites the two peninsular capitals, makes it famous to-day. Its bullring brings many sad memories to older folk in the city. That was the place where much blood was shed during the Spanish civil war. Matadors were no longer killing innocent bulls but instead thousands of innocent people, many of whose relatives still live today. Estimates range from 5,000 - 15,000.

At first we couldn't help comparing it to the beautiful city of Córdoba where we had first lived in Spain. That made us aware of all the imperfections and poverty of this city that seemed to us rather ugly at first sight.

However we began to pray earnestly for the city and its wellbeing as exhorted in Jeremiah 29:7 'And seek the peace of the city ...and pray unto the Lord for it.' With the years we could see more and more improvements being made and when we left in 2013, we could truly say we had fallen in love with it and its people. The Arabic castle, the 13th century cathedral, the impressive city entrance gate at Puerta de Palmas, and the Archaeological Museum have all been cleaned up. Tourists now visit the city. Perhaps the most significant change is the opening up of the Plaza Alta in the old part of the city. When we arrived, we were told not to go into that part.

'It is much too dangerous and known for its robberies by all the drug addicts and gypsies who live there' we were told.

Desmond however ignored that. Perhaps he thought our experience with gypsies and drug addicts in Córdoba had taught us all we needed to know about those marginalised members of society. The town council spent a lot of money to renovate the old square and now it has several prestigious bars and restaurants. We enjoyed sitting in the open air and admiring the architecture. Badajoz even has its own small airport with flights to Madrid and Barcelona and to Mallorca in the summer months.

One of the couples who had left us in Córdoba to start their own church (mentioned in chapter 13) found it was not so easy and in fact the church closed down after a few years. They had come to visit us in the UK and it was a wonderful time of reconciliation. We were able to forgive them and they wanted to make amends for what they had done. The husband was a kitchen fitter and he promised that if ever we came back to Spain, he would help us with our kitchen. At that time rented flats came without any kitchen furniture. Julian kept his promise, taking us to a large warehouse where we could choose and buy kitchen furniture with a good discount. He then came for a few days to put it in for us at no cost. That was such a blessing.

OUR FIRST MEETINGS. It was a strange feeling to be in a city with scarcely anyone we knew and we had to battle with loneliness. We soon connected with the group of young people we had met in the park the year before and began to have meetings in our flat each week as soon as we arrived. Not all the young folk wanted to commit themselves but some did and especially Paco, mentioned in the previous chapter. We celebrated our first baptism service for him in the open air in a dam in Portugal. What we didn't realise was that he was HIV positive and he was most reluctant to tell us about this. A famous singer had encouraged a lot of young unemployed men like himself to go to work in bars in Seville. There he was introduced to the homosexual lifestyle. Now he had come back to his family in Badajoz, quite repentant but suffering the consequences in his health.

Through Paco we were able to learn a lot about AIDS and the horrible death that its sufferers have. We watched him get thinner and thinner until his bones stood out terribly all over his body. By the time he died, his family hardly came to visit him. They were just too ashamed. A nurse actually asked me in hospital one day if I was a relative since I seemed to her to be the only regular visitor. Of course, it was not a very pleasant experience as we had to wear masks and the smell was extremely hard to bear. By this time, we did have a church and some of the South American members who had never known Paco much did visit him faithfully until the end. I do admire them for that as not much was known about the disease then and folk were very suspicious of it and its dangers to others.

CONNECTIONS WITH CÓRDOBA. In June 1993 we had a lovely experience connecting us again with all our friends from Córdoba. Our first convert from those days, Marie Pili Sanchiz, was getting married to Jan, a Dutch man working with YWAM in Seville. Desmond was invited to preach at the wedding which was held in the open air in one of the most beautiful hotels in the city. Since Marie Pili was an art teacher whose father was a famous sculptor called Aurelio, the wedding was a most artistic affair. The seven-tiered wedding cake was a work of art. Once again, I was glad to be back in this country of artistic people. As someone once said if Spain had as many economists or scientists as it has artists and musicians, it would be a very prosperous country!

MY SPECIAL FRIEND. I often wondered about the prophecy I had received about the special friend I was to have in the block of flats. I decided I would not force anything to form a friendship but just watch things happen. Soon a dear lady, Paquita, on the first floor, began to come up to visit me. She would bring little presents of flowers, plants and fruit from their fruit farm in the valley of 'El Jerte' in Extremadura. I had watched this lady go out to shop each week at the market in her real fur coat and leather gloves. Spanish ladies do believe in dressing up and especially the older ones. She soon became that special friend. Since we were in rented accommodation, she was very concerned about the lack of shine on my marble floor and began to show me how to make it shine. She and her husband sometimes took us to stay in the country with their elderly relatives where we admired the cherry blossom so famous in that area.

In fact, she seemed to so appreciate my friendship that when her mother died, she insisted that I walk beside her arm in arm. There I was parading behind the hearse through the village for all to see and I remembered my anti-Catholic friends and relatives in Northern Ireland. What would they think? Paquita said I transmitted such peace that she preferred to have me close rather than her two sisters on that occasion. That friendship continued for our twenty years in the city and proved to be important when

WEDDING OF JAN AND MARI-PILI

we were later looking for a church building. The family was able to rent us out a suitable warehouse at a low rent for many years.

A Catholic sort of YWAM group which operated from Malta visited Badajoz a few times. I invited Paquita to one of their meetings. As they prayed for her, they asked me to join in. This I thought was very open of them since they knew we were planting a Protestant church in the city. Paquita was powerfully touched.

A SAD EXPERIENCE. We had a sad experience in those early days in Badajoz. Estela, who had been converted with us in England, had by now a boyfriend Toni who was a student at the local university. He decided to become a Christian and attend Estela's church. We were delighted as we could see he was very introverted and suffered continually with depressive thoughts. We did what we could to help him, especially when Estela decided to finish her relationship with him. He arrived at our flat very distraught and we made a decision to invite him to stay the night with us. The next day Desmond was going off to another part of the country to work and we thought it would not be a good witness to the neighbours if this young man were to stay alone in the flat with me. Rumours fly around easily about foreign missionaries and we didn't want to spoil our reputation, new in the city as we were.

Two days later, we received an anxious phone call from Estela, asking if we had seen Toni. Her brother had been to his flat but got no reply either from his door or from his phone. After some hours Estela and her brother decided to go to the flat and open the door with the key she still had. Fortunately, her brother went in first and found to his horror the dead body of Toni who had hanged himself in the entrance hall. Estela was saved from that sight. However, she was not saved from the horrible publicity that followed. The radio and newspaper journalists were soon on the scene. They demanded interviews with this 17 year old girl who had broken up with her boyfriend 48 hours before he killed himself! Estela was the one to find her own father dead in the bathroom when only 13, so you can imagine the effect the death of Toni now had on her. She clung to Desmond who had to be with her in all the interviews with the press. She was plagued with guilt and condemnation as we all were to a lesser degree. *Could we not have avoided this somehow?* This was hardly the glorious beginning to the church in Badajoz that we had expected. I should add that Estela is now happily married to a medical specialist in Mexico.

Another couple joined us from the Pentecostal church. What we did not realise was that this was a very problematic couple and in fact the husband soon told us he was really a homosexual. His wife could not have an intimate relationship with him. They brought a brother and wife and another friend to our meetings. They were both married but also with homosexual tendencies and had been attending the Jehovah Witness meetings. What a complicated bunch with which to begin a church! We worked for some time with these three couples but in the end, it all came to nothing. One even demanded from us all the tithes he had given during the year. We gave these to him of course but again were left rather deflated.

What about all the promising prophecies we had received before returning to Spain? We were certainly not seeing all the quick answers to our prayers like we had seen upon arriving in Córdoba those many years before. Disappointment had to be dealt with.

18 EARLY ATTEMPTS TO PLANT A CHURCH

CHRISTIAN SCHOOL VISITS. I was still in close contact with some Christian schools back in the UK. Groups of pupils came from these schools in Basingstoke, Harpenden, Gloucester and Bangor (Northern Ireland) to have an experience of mission. We offered help with English classes in the local schools during the morning and a sort of pre-evangelistic programme in English at lunch time. Some schools refused to have us as they regarded anything non-Catholic as a sect. However, the teachers in the Catholic schools we entered were particularly impressed by the teenage pupils. They asked me

'How do you ever produce these healthy and obviously spiritual young people? How is it that they are happy to express their Christian faith in public and are not turned off by the church?'

They were concerned about the number of Catholic teenagers who were leaving church and all their Catholic upbringing. These visits were well received and we had special reception times with the mayor and even TV coverage. One of the children from Harpenden said that as he prayed he had something of a vision.

'I saw a big event in a conference hall with lots of buses arriving'.

That was encouraging and we remembered it years later when it actually happened.

OUR ENGLISH LIBRARY AND RESOURCE CENTRE. Maruja had kindly rented us a flat of hers where we set up an English Library and Resource Centre. English Christians had collected lots of books for us and some had even made visual aids for English classes. I had prepared material for teachers of English after seeing how few resources they had in their schools. We had advertised it in the local schools and young people began to visit it and use the opportunity to chat in English to the English student there. For a small fee Spaniards could also use the internet. This was in the days before cyber cafes had arrived in Badajoz. Several students had come out from the UK and even the USA, to help us man the resource centre. They also offered their services free to schools. In this way we were becoming known in the city and making our presence felt.

MAKING NEW FRIENDS. How do you begin a church in a new city? We had spent a lot of time making friends and relationships wherever we could. Anthony and Susan had a second child by now with golden blond hair and these children attracted attention. Three middle class couples stood out so we began to meet occasionally with them for Bible studies. This went well and all seemed to experience God but went back into the Catholic church, which was more socially acceptable. There they found openings to serve. They remained good friends and in fact later helped find work for many of our Latin American immigrants.

EXPERIENCE AT A SCOUT LEADERS' RETREAT. In the first few years we were invited to represent the Protestant church at a national Scout leaders' retreat. We had got to know the local scout leader in Badajoz and, although we had never been in the scout movement ourselves, he decided we could fit the role. The subject was 'spiritual values among youth' and there was a Catholic priest and a Spanish Muslim also invited from the large mosque in Madrid. Desmond was given the privilege of speaking first.

To finish his talk, he shared a tape of Estela giving the testimony of her conversion and how God had helped her after the suicide of her ex-boyfriend.

The Muslim had brought two Arabs with him and I could see all three were getting more and more furious as Desmond spoke. The Muslim then spoke and proved to be an excellent orator. He didn't keep to the subject at all and instead gave a very clever talk about how we should all convert to Islam as he had. The Catholic priest was so nervous as he had to follow him that when he finished his talk he gave me an enormous hug before he sat down. We had not met this priest before and I was not used to hugs from Catholic priests. Those I had met before were always more cautious and bowed to kiss my hand. This one wanted to thank me for how my husband, in his opinion, had not been afraid to tell the truth.

We both suddenly remembered a prophecy given to us many years before in Londonderry by our dear friend Stanley. We were to meet a fanatical Muslim in Spain but we were not to be alarmed as God would protect us. We certainly experienced that at the retreat. I was convinced that the Scout leaders would be keen to talk to the Muslims at the meal table afterwards, but no. Nobody went near them and instead many came to our table both then and the next morning to ask questions. I was reminded once more of Proverbs 2:6-7 'For the Lord giveth wisdom: out of his mouth cometh knowledge and understanding. He lays up sound wisdom for the righteous: he is a buckler to them that walk uprightly.' The human wisdom of the Muslim had not convinced the vulnerable young Scout leaders after all.

ALPHA. On a visit back to the UK we had shared on the same platform as Nicky Gumbel from Holy Trinity Brompton Church, London. He gave us a copy of Alpha (an evangelistic course which seeks to introduce the basics of the Christian faith) and details of how to get it in Spanish, which we did. Imagine our surprise when a friend came to show us a copy of a well-known esoteric magazine 'Más Allá'- Nu.81/11/95. There was a very positive and long article by J.C. Deus. This young Spaniard had visited Holy Trinity Brompton and seen for himself the effect of the Toronto blessing. This term was coined by British newspapers to describe the revival and resulting phenomena that began at Toronto Airport Christian Fellowship in 1994. He concluded that what he had seen was authentic compared with what he had been brought up with in Catholicism. The Holy Spirit he thought was the missing link making this church more like the church 2,000 years before. Alpha was mentioned too and a couple of British Missionaries (we ourselves!) living in Badajoz who along with a church in Zaragoza were the contacts in Spain for the course. We never expected to get a mention in such a magazine. God used these little things to encourage us.

ENCOURAGEMENT FROM ENGLAND. However, we were frustrated as we seemed to be no nearer to our goal of a church plant. Four years had passed by and Anthony and Susan, who had come with us, told us their time had finished in Badajoz. With a heavy heart we watched them leave. We fasted and prayed and even wondered if our time too had not come to leave. If it had not been for all the encouragement from Edwin and Margaret Monger and their regular visits to us with teams from the UK, we probably would have thrown in the towel. These teams were mostly made up of older Christians who certainly knew how to pray and intercede for a strong church to be established in the city. For one team Desmond had organised meals in a Spanish restaurant at midday. Though we were well used to Spanish food and its greasiness at times, we forgot that this was very difficult for the English. They had nicknamed the restaurant 'Greasy Joe!' and really struggled with the traditional Spanish menu that was on offer.

We read and re-read all the promising prophecies we had received. Piedy Palmer in prayer had seen angels marching around the city and the following year had seen them marching with us into the city. We were reminded about one prophecy in particular. It spoke about the sense of siege about the city like Wellington's assault during the Peninsular War. This was a bloody and hard fight but the Iron Duke won in the end.

'I think your visit to the city is going to be victorious but it will be a hard fight' were the final words of the prophecy we received.

We walked around the walls of Badajoz, praying and remembering Wellington's fight and victory many times. We even read the books by Bernard Cornwell about Richard Sharpe, the fictional British soldier in the Napoleonic Wars. Most English people had never heard of Badajoz until the television series based on his books was shown in the UK a few years after our arrival in the city.

We returned to the UK for a conference and one evening my husband felt so low he couldn't go to the meeting. Instead he prayed in the hotel room and God spoke to him. He said

'It is no longer maintenance mode but time for outreach mode'.

He wrestled with God, asking where the human and financial resources were. The company he had worked with at the beginning was proving to be unsuitable for the small firms in Extremadura. Any sales he had made were in other parts of Spain such as Madrid, Barcelona, Victoria or Valencia where businesses were large, but these meant long tiring journeys by car. It was not uncommon to arrive for a meeting after a six or eight hour drive and be told that the director had to go to another meeting! Once his car was broken into and all his business files were stolen from the boot. All this travelling was defeating the purpose of our living in Badajoz so other work had to be found. From time to time he got work as an interpreter in business conferences and I was teaching English to the neighbours but we were just about getting by each month.

TEACHING A FUTURE MATADOR. One pupil stands out, though not exactly for his progress with English. In fact, he struggled so much and became quite envious of another pupil in his group. His reaction was to punch the other lad until he had a black eye, as soon as they left our flat.

'Take that' he shouted at him.

After that his mother had to come and collect him each time from the class. It was no surprise to hear years later that this boy became quite a famous young matador in the area.

SETTING UP ENGLISH ACADEMIES. A pupil from Olivenza, a nearby town, had opened the way for us to begin the first English academy there and introduced us to all the right influential people. Olivenza with its 10,000 inhabitants was very picturesque and its architecture was mainly Portuguese. In fact, throughout history it was often disputed whether it actually belonged to Spain or Portugal. As recently as 1995 the Portuguese administration did not consider Olivenza as part of Spain. The academy that opened there in the spring of 1997 was making money but we had to hire a teacher to help us there which ate up most of our profits. Jenny Slater came from a New Frontiers International Church in England. We returned to Badajoz, waiting to see what God would do. Having had this experience with academies, we then decided to open one in another town called Villanueva de la Serena. This was to help an English missionary couple who were struggling financially. Once opened the couple continued to run the academy on their own.

BEGINNING OF MEETINGS IN PRESBYTERIAN CHURCH. Desmond was given a job by the local Chamber of Commerce to help businesses in Extremadura export their goods from time to time. A friend of Maruja's who happened to work there, recommended him. We were learning the importance of relationships in Spain. It is not so much what you know as who you know that can get you a job in that country. Shortly things turned around. In three months he earned more than he had earned in the previous three years! God was providing the financial resources we needed.

Phil Berry and his wife Jo from *World Horizons* mission decided to come to work with us and at our invitation to live in Olivenza with their family. They worked with us for a few years and took over the teaching of the pupils from our academy there. The well-known mission *Latin Link International* later contacted us to ask if we would receive someone from their mission to help in our church plant. For some reason, which I can't now remember, that never actually happened. However we realised that God was providing the human resources we needed for any sort of outreach.

We approached the Spanish Presbyterian minister who had a large church building in the centre of the town and only two members. The building was old and in much need of repair but the minister was happy to let us use it once a month. Our first event was to hold a public discussion about the recently published joint document produced by the Lutheran and Catholic churches on justification by faith. Desmond and a Catholic priest were the speakers. The hall was packed and we were encouraged, even though we discovered a large drip in the middle of the hall due to a hole in the roof.

'Help. What can we do now?' we said.

The drip and the rain however stopped just before folks arrived which left me with a conviction that God was on our side.

We had several more events and then began a weekly meeting in the church building together with the Presbyterian minister and his wife. Latin American immigrants came as well as some from Eastern European countries. These were usually in great financial need and we did what we could to help them. I remember coming home one day, rather horrified to find Desmond had invited a

OUR FLAT-TOP RIGHT

crowd of these immigrants for a meal and the cooking was well underway. One young man from the Ukraine had a degree in Economics and Business Studies and was convinced that Desmond could help him.

'Please' he pleaded with us, 'I really need a job.'

He had just discovered that Desmond had his own business. He needed this to be able to act as an export consultant and interpret at conferences on occasions. My English classes came under the umbrella of his business. Unfortunately, we couldn't offer this man any work and he went off saddened to another town. About a year later we heard that he had committed suicide in a fit of despair as he was still unable to find work. Another life we had touched but not successfully!

Suddenly the Presbyterian minister decided to stop the joint meeting without any reason. We were shocked but fortunately that afternoon we were meeting up with the other two Protestant pastors of the town with their wives. They were all Spaniards and we enjoyed some good times together of fellowship and fun. They immediately encouraged us in our situation and one even offered us a place to store things we had to get out of the Presbyterian building.

BACK TO CHURCH IN OUR NEWLY BOUGHT FLAT. We had to go back to holding meetings in our flat. By this time, we had decided to put down our roots in Badajoz and buy our own flat. We had got to know a lovely Catholic charismatic couple, Enrique and his wife, who told us about a flat they were selling. It was on the tenth floor of the highest apartment block in the city which meant it had lovely views. They had held lots of prayer meetings in the flat and wanted that to continue so they offered it to us. The actual sale was most unusual. We sat in our lounge singing worship songs while I played the piano and we agreed on a price together.

To our surprise we managed to get a mortgage but at the last minute we realised we were £1,000 short. Enrique gave us a year to pay back that extra money and we moved in. A few days later Enrique came to collect the last of his belongings from the house and a letter arrived at the same time from our old friend Alwyn Harland. Inside was a cheque for £1,000. He stipulated that this was only to be used to buy our flat and if we didn't need it for that his instructions were to return the cheque! Enrique simply shrugged his shoulders and said

'I knew God would provide the money for you!'

What a confirmation that we were in God's paths!

19 INFLUX OF LATIN AMERICANS

THE FIRST COLOMBIANS. Ruby wasn't exactly a spring chicken. She was an elderly Colombian lady who had come to accompany her unmarried son, a lecturer at Badajoz university. Ruby became a good friend and her son who was very intellectual started coming to our meetings as well. Her grandson also came over for three months. The lecturer appeared to be seeking God and his mother was delighted. However, we were soon to discover the great divide between the classes that is so obvious in Latin America compared with Europe. When other more working-class Colombians arrived he simply did not want to mix with them in such a close setting. Instead he became merely a friend whom we saw from time to time. His mother eventually became ill and went back to Colombia. This was after some folk from our church had looked after her at no small cost to themselves.

ARRIVAL OF OSCAR, OUR EVANGELIST. A few Latin Americans had come to our last meetings in the Presbyterian building and obviously spread the word about us. As a result, we received a phone call from a young Colombian who was destined to be very significant in our church plant. Oscar had been on the point of moving into drug trafficking when his life was dramatically changed after an encounter with God in Colombia. Two weeks later he decided to emigrate to Spain and came to Don Benito in Extremadura where his partner from a four-year relationship was living. It was a shock for him to find that Luz Denia had fallen back into prostitution as in her teenage years. He had tried to find a Protestant church there but couldn't. The Protestant churches in Extremadura are few and far between and often not well advertised. This was so different to our experience in Latin America where we seemed to find them at every corner!

When Oscar heard we were in the process of starting a church in Badajoz, he came to visit us and immediately decided

'I want to move here to help you.'

He was so pleased and relieved to find Christians that he wept loudly. We knew little about this stocky young man with his winsome smile. Yet both my husband and I had a strong conviction that we should offer him accommodation with us until he found his own flat. Others were quick to point out the dangers and how we could get into trouble with the police but we decided we were meant to take the risk. This incident is described in chapter one. A week later he had found his own flat which Desmond signed for.

At that stage no one was renting out to Latin Americans unless they had a guarantor. What we didn't expect was the arrival of two plain clothed police detectives at our door a few hours later. He wanted to find out more about this young Colombian who was living with us. I answered the door and panicked I must confess. *Had we made a big mistake? Was Oscar a criminal on the run? Was he a drug smuggler or a terrorist?* The warnings of other missionaries still rang in my ears. Fortunately, Desmond arrived home at that moment and assured the men

'Yes, we do know Oscar Ramiro. Yes, he is staying with us and no, he isn't a danger to society'.

The detectives went off satisfied.

LUZ DENIA WAS TO FOLLOW. Oscar became like a son to us. He took up the vision for a church and began to bring more and more Colombians to our meetings. He was a natural evangelist. The first to be converted was his partner, Luz Denia, who came to visit us. Luz Denia was an attractive young woman working in a club in Don Benito. There she was earning a lot of money to send back to her mother in Colombia who was looking after her two children. She had a real encounter with God in our home that day which caused her to question her present lifestyle. I was very delighted about that since I had always wanted to rescue folk from prostitution ever since living for a month with the couple of pastors in Switzerland who did just that. We all realised it would be best for her to move to Badajoz and start afresh.

It was very humbling for her to find a job near us as a 'live-in' maid in uniform with an elderly lady. There she was treated basically as a slave and paid a very low salary. She was very ashamed of her past and reluctant to tell us much about it for a long time. Little by little her story came out amidst her sobs.

'I had my first child when I was fifteen and then I got into the drug world. My family was very poor so I was lured into prostitution and even taken to Japan for a while in that same profession. Three years later I had a second child and the father of the child died in my arms as a result of drug abuse. A short time afterwards my own father died in my arms as well. This was the result of terrorist fighting in Colombia'.

We spent a lot of time praying and counselling her and little by little she experienced a lot of healing of her emotions. In fact, I had to teach her a bit of everything, how to save money on her housekeeping and even how to dress so as not to draw so many men around her. She often told me

'You have taught me more than ever my mother taught me'.

'It sounded like angels singing!' said Luz Denia breathlessly.

Where was it coming from? The street was empty. Doors and windows were closed. Nobody was about. She was desperately missing her two children and one day she was in the street in Badajoz thinking a lot about them. Suddenly she heard music like an angelic choir and a voice said to her

'If only you will have faith as a grain of mustard seed'.

The following Sunday in church a Spanish school teacher who was a bachelor approached her. He said he believed he was meant to pay the fares for her to go back to Colombia and bring over her two children, aged six and nine. You can imagine the emotion for her and indeed for us too. In the end she was unable to return on the same flight as her children and Desmond had to go to Madrid airport to collect them. They arrived, quite happily munching sweets given to them by the air hostesses. That was the first wonderful family reunion we were able to be part of. There were to be many more as we prayed for other families to be reunited.

FINDING OUR UPPER ROOM. Oscar and Luz Denia brought so many people to the meetings in our flat that we soon realised we needed to look for other premises. They got there before us and in fact after visiting various agencies they found us a suite of offices on the first floor of a building not far from the centre. We called it our 'upper room' and indeed many were filled with the Spirit there just as in the book of Acts. At a wedding for two Colombians, we even got about 80 people into the meeting room and fed them too.

We were thrilled with the arrival of the Latin Americans. God spoke to us from the scriptures about how to treat the foreigners and aliens: Deuteronomy 10:17-19; Deuteronomy 24:19-21; Exodus 23:9; Psalm 146:9. We endeavoured to obey and show them all the love we could. I used to go with the women to job interviews and my presence sometimes gave confidence to employers who were unsure about having foreigners to work in their homes. Desmond was able to get work for some of them in a factory where he had been an export consultant. We prayed and somehow many found jobs. In fact, this happened so much that folk began to arrive at our meetings saying that they were told to come here as we could get them jobs! One Cuban English graduate was convinced that we were the owners of the factory and thus got jobs for folks there! That was the only way her natural mind could explain all the answers to prayer.

THE REAL CHURCH BEGINS. At last we could really begin our church in Badajoz after several false starts. We felt very much like David in 1 Samuel 22:1-2 'and everyone that was in distress, and everyone that was in debt, and everyone that was discontented, gathered themselves unto him'. 2 Samuel 23 encouraged us of course when we read how these men became David's mighty men of valour. We had also been greatly encouraged by a prophetic picture someone in the UK had for us. They saw an enormous fierce bull with its horns chasing a tiny mouse. Then the picture changed and the mouse was chasing the bull. We no longer had a walking stick but were using a two-edged sword and became powerful warriors in the land of the matador.

'A plant has been planted and it will grow high', were the exact words. 'Many will come to you and ask, how has this thing been?'

Our first baptismal service of the Latin Americans is one I will not easily forget because I never actually got there. We planned it out in the country at a river as often happens in Spain. Two

THE ENTRANCE TO OUR CHURCH BUILDING,
BEFORE (above) AFTER (below-made by Desmond)

Colombian ladies recently converted in our meetings came to our flat that morning. They were very distressed as the landlord had suddenly evicted them and they told us

'We have to have all our belongings out by midday. Where can we go?'

Although I desperately wanted to be at the baptisms of Oscar, Luz Denia and others, I knew I had to help these two ladies in their time of need.

I remember the seething crowd of neighbours around their flat that morning. They were shouting

'We don't want such foreigners here'.

They were seemingly bringing in all sorts of men at nights. The police were actually involved in bringing out the belongings and setting them down in the street. I went to speak to the police, introducing myself as a minister's wife and told them that these two at least were cleaning up their lives and I believed had been transformed.

'Keep you out of this' they shouted in their anger.

There was nothing left to do but pick up their belongings and take them to our flat until they found other accommodation. I suddenly realised what it was like to hear that dreadful racist spirit come against two ladies whom God loved and did not despise despite their dubious past.

ANOTHER STEP OF FAITH TO NEW PREMISES. It was soon time to find bigger premises and we found a derelict warehouse which we rented at a low price from our former neighbours (Paquita's family). Around the same time the Presbyterian minister came to us to ask if we wanted to buy his building. This was the one well-known Protestant church building in the city. However, we had no means of finance and the building while in a good position, needed a lot of repairs. It was rather sad to watch the building being sold to a theatre company, but we were given the two large wooden crosses and a door with special glass windows as well as the wooden pews. This was a great help for our warehouse for which the rent was double the price we had been paying for the last premises and thus a big step of faith for us.

Moreover, we had to put in a kitchen and toilets, including one for disabled and all this cost a lot of money.

My husband did most of the work helped by our members of course. He even made a large wooden front door to make the building more 'church like'. Appearances are so important in Spain. Once again God was faithful and somehow the money came in to pay the rent for the first month. We all rejoiced, knowing that while our members were very faithful in paying their tithe to the church, none of them had a high wage. Desmond and another church member decided to run a half marathon from Olivenza castle to Badajoz castle, a distance of some twenty five kilometres, and got sponsors for the run. We also got a lot of publicity in the local press. Even the regional TV channel got interested. They aired a fifteen minute interview with Desmond and then sent a cameraman to film the run at 7 am (a very early hour for Spain!). Sponsored runs were a novelty in July 2002 in Spain and 'a Protestant priest running in the heat of the summer to get money for his church' was quite unheard of.

ROMANCE AMONG THE IMMIGRANTS. One thing we never expected, when we began to work with immigrants in Spain, was to become so involved in their romances, love triangles and separations. However, they explained to us that here they were in a foreign country far away from family and family is still quite a close unit in Latin America. The natural response was then to look on us, their church ministers, as their family, their 'Mum and Dad' to give a bit of guidance from time to time.

Oscar still loved Luz Denia yet she was unsure about him because he seemed so indecisive and she by this stage was looking for a father for her two children. A friend of hers encouraged her to go to work in Barcelona and we wondered if we would ever see her again, but she did come back quite repentant. In a bar one day she met another Colombian who fell in love with her and soon took her and her two children to live with him in Antequera. However, she separated from him after six months and came back to Badajoz.

Oscar, now 26, had been extremely jealous and upset about this relationship and poured out his heart to us at times. Eventually she met Enrique. Enrique had been dragged to church by his seven-year-old daughter who had been coming with her carer. She used to recite scriptures that she had learnt by heart with her grandmother. Her own mother was a high-class prostitute in Badajoz. This child would sometimes repeat what she had seen her mother do; that is offer massages to any men who gave her attention! Enrique, slim, handsome and full of energy, had always refused to come to church until he had a serious car accident where he almost lost his life. He was converted and became Luz Denia's husband and we performed our first wedding in Badajoz.

What a memorable day! We had to take on many different roles. I went to help dress the bride that morning and the seam and several buttons burst at the last minute. Sewing is not exactly one of my gifts but it is wonderful what we can do in an emergency. Her two sisters arrived from the north of Spain for the wedding at the last minute. Instead of encouraging her at that important moment of her life, they began to tell her how awful she looked in that dress. They themselves were both living with Spaniards but not married. She burst into tears and I had a job consoling her. Then Desmond drove her off to the church in our car, suitably decorated with ribbon and balloons. While photographs were taken at the church door, Desmond quickly got ready to take the church ceremony. They could not afford to take holidays from their jobs to have a honeymoon so our wedding present to them was a night in a hotel without their children. This they really appreciated.

Enrique and Oscar actually became good friends, though for some years we could see their jealousy of one another. Little did we imagine that Enrique and Luz Denia years later would become the first pastors from our work in that city.

Oscar also had plenty of admirers. In fact, one gypsy lady we had who was our prayer secretary was so convinced that he was to be her husband that she left the church. She had realised it was not going to happen. It was a relief when he finally married in May 2007. Evangelist as he was, he wanted to preach at his own wedding and my husband finally agreed to a five minute slot at the end. Sure enough he made an appeal and several responded. They look back on that day as the day they met with God.

GETTING TO KNOW ALL THE DIFFERENT LATINOS. Folk began to arrive from all parts of Latin America and we had fun trying to understand all the different accents and even vocabulary. The Brazilians were the most difficult since they came to work in nearby Portugal and most didn't think they needed to learn Spanish. There was one family in particular who made lots of money by bringing over Brazilian footballers and lived themselves in a beautiful block of flats with its own swimming pool. Soon when the church members were beginning to enjoy the use of their pool, they moved away to another city. The Brazilians spoke what was sometimes called portuñol, a mixture of the two languages. Years later I got so frustrated with trying to understand them that I began to attend Portuguese classes myself. I remembered how years before in a ladies' meeting in Basingstoke, I had been challenged to take up a new challenge. That challenge I knew for me even then was to learn another language.

Diana arrived from Colombia and was absolutely traumatised. Her pastor, a married man, had fallen madly in love with her. He wanted to elope with her and had bought her some very expensive gifts. She resisted and escaped to Spain instead. We had to pray a lot with her. The final breakthrough came when she and I took all of these gifts and burnt them on the outskirts of the town. She is now happily married to a man from the Dominican Republic. Some of these Latin Americans like Diana came from churches already but most such as her future husband were converted with us. Many of the immigrants just passed through for a year or two and then moved on to another town in the hope of a better job. Others took very seriously their commitment to our church and stayed with us. Oscar in particular refused some good jobs because he put God and His church in first place. Others moved from the more traditional churches in the town because they said they felt more in a family with us.

At Christmas time I cooked my turkey in the traditional British way and took it down to the church for those without family to come and join us. This became more and more popular and others then began to bring food typical of their country at that season. In later years we had a bigger house and were able to invite folks to our home instead of the church building. The immigrants were often in tears, expressing at the end of the evening their surprise at being able to have such a happy Christmas away from family and loved ones. We ourselves look back on those times with pleasure. It is truly 'more blessed to give than to receive.' Acts 20:35.

Oscar was particularly generous to others. Since his job was night watchman, he used to offer his bed to several new immigrants who got up when he came in from work to go to bed. His mother then came from Colombia to live with him and help him run what had almost become a rescue mission in his small flat before he got married.

RELATIONSHIPS WITH THE CATHOLIC CHURCH. A pastor's wife in the UK once prayed a very powerful prayer for us. She prayed that God would open those dark wooden doors for us into churches. What she didn't realise was that Protestant churches don't normally have that type of door. Catholic churches do. From our early days in Badajoz we had good relationships with Catholics. Many would ask us if the Catholic church was our biggest opposition in the work in Spain, but we didn't really find it so.

We attended some conferences run by Catholic charismatic groups in Extremadura and were made very welcome. We were surprised to hear public testimonies given of 'conversion experiences' and their emphasis on Bible study and the gifts of the Spirit. The leader knelt down in front of us and asked Desmond to pray for him. At the end all were asked to turn around and pray to the Virgin Mary. This we couldn't do but as the leader quickly assured us

'Please just join in the things we have in common'.

A Catholic priest once invited us to come to speak to some of his leaders about the involvement of lay people in the church. It was a great privilege to be able to open the scriptures and talk about how we saw the church of the New Testament. Then we began to get invitations to take part in a joint meeting of Catholics and Protestants in Badajoz. Desmond at first was the only

RELATIONS WITH THE CATHOLIC CHURCH.
RADIO AND TELEVISION INTERVIEWS
WERE REGULAR EVENTS

Protestant pastor willing to go to these meetings. The others, who had been brought up in the Catholic church and then left it, had suffered a lot. They couldn't bring themselves to go back.

We clearly explained that we didn't think the two churches would ever unite but we were happy to share in meetings together. We shared stories of reconciliation that we had experienced in Northern Ireland many years before. We believed we were following in the steps of Paul who always went to preach the gospel where there was an audience willing to listen. This may have been the Jewish synagogue or a place of prayer beside the river or the Areopagus at Athens. We were often impressed at how intently the people listened in the Catholic churches. We got the impression they were hanging on to our every word, whereas in some Protestant churches the folk were at times quite restless.

In Catholic countries like Spain, as I have already said, anything that is not Catholic is considered a sect and folk are very suspicious of it. We found it broke down a lot of barriers when talking to people to be able to say that Desmond had preached in a Catholic church or been on the Catholic radio and TV. People relaxed before our eyes. In fact, we had a lot of opposition from neighbours in the block when we first began our meetings in the warehouse. Then when the Catholic Archbishop came to one of our meetings, they were amazed and even queued up to get in. At last we were accepted.

The archbishops showed us great respect and the first one we met said to Desmond

'Please feel free to come and share with me both your joys and your sorrows.'

This we never actually did but when we needed larger premises for joint church meetings it was useful to be able to contact him and use their well-equipped buildings. We had a few opportunities to share with nuns from a closed order in Badajoz. I once gave them a worship CD from Mexico which they really appreciated and asked for more.

The Catholic TV asked if they could televise our service and were very considerate to our requests. They only gave us a day's warning and I pointed out that the walls were not painted yet in certain places. They kindly said they wouldn't put the cameras on those parts. They televised Oscar giving his testimony and didn't attempt to shorten it or cut anything important from our service. This was in contrast to the local commercial TV who years later asked to come and televise our Christmas service.

Little was actually shown of the service, only a snippet of me leading worship, Desmond preaching and some Latin American faces in the congregation. They were more interested in showing that Protestant churches were for foreigners, exactly the opposite of the image we wanted to portray.

LESSONS LEARNED FROM THE LATINOS. Someone once said that anyone engaged in church work has to be a shock absorber; absorbing all the complaints and moans about what people dislike in church and also be a general dog's body. At times I did feel like that. Another preacher said that we had to have the hide of a rhinoceros and the heart of a dove. In other words we have to learn how to toughen our hide without hardening our heart. We certainly have to die daily and often pray as Jesus did 'Not my will but thine be done'.

The Latin Americans who had come from large churches in their own countries couldn't understand why the churches in Spain were so small. They all wanted to tell Desmond and me how we should be running the church, how it was done in Colombia, Bolivia, Brazil, Uruguay, Paraguay, Costa Rica, Mexico, Dominican Republic, Ecuador or Peru. While we listened, we had to explain that we were running a church for Spaniards and sought always to be led by the direction we received from God and our pastors from the UK confirming it. I later discovered that this was happening in other churches too, so once I wrote a play about it. We performed it at a weekend retreat for pastors' wives and missionaries and we all laughed a lot. Proverbs 17:22 was becoming a reality as we learnt the importance of laughter as good medicine for us all. I quote from the Amplified Bible 'A happy heart is good medicine and a cheerful mind works healing'.

We learnt so much from those Latin Americans. They often lived in cramped conditions, several families in one small flat when they first arrived, yet were so generous. They showed us such respect and honour. We were always given lavish helpings of food and wondered why the others were not sitting at the meal table with us. We soon realised that they didn't have enough chairs for everyone or even plates so they themselves would only eat later.

I remember a family from Peru, delighted to have found a flat for themselves. They insisted on having the house group there to see it. I wondered why the drinks were taking so long to be served. Then I realised that they only had five glasses for both coffee and cold drinks so they were being continually washed before the others could be served. As Europeans we would be embarrassed and apologetic finding ourselves in that situation but not them. They were keen to share what they had. In fact, I have never received so many presents as I have received from Latin Americans. They just love to give, no matter how poor they are.

They were mostly full of faith as well which was a real example for us in Europe. They knew what it was to trust God to get papers to stay in Spain. We used to be horrified when they told us

'We have come into the country as tourists yet we have faith we can somehow get a job and thus permission to stay on in the country'.

Numerous times we saw God honour their faith and provide the job and papers just at the last minute.

One Colombian man working as a baker, broke his arm. This was disastrous for him since he was without papers and thus unable to claim any sickness benefit. *How would he and his children eat?* He came to us for prayer. After the prayer his arm hurt so badly that he went to the hospital. They took the plaster off and gave him an X-ray. No sign of fracture or breakages could be seen on his arm! They were so grateful for the health service in Spain after having to pay for medicine, doctors and hospitals. I found them also so knowledgeable about simple remedies.

They are used to having a special 'Appreciation' day for their pastors and one was organised for us as a big surprise. We were told not to come to church by car as usual as someone would collect us. In true 'Latino' style they came late and we had no idea why. We arrived at the church to find an arcade of our members all cheering us. The women were holding up red roses and the men their Bibles, making an impressive long archway for us to walk through. When we got in, we found a large screen with our son and grandson greeting us from the UK. This was followed by some slides from our childhood and lots of food as always. A special cake had been made with a church, two shepherds and some sheep on the top tier. We were given two different presents by the congregation as well as flowers, again showing their tremendous generosity. On another occasion we were preaching in a Brazilian church (Pentecostal Wesleyan) that actually had this day firmly fixed in their church calendar. While the main presents were presented to their pastors, we were also given a lovely plant to show their appreciation to us too.

20 SOME REMARKABLE COLOMBIANS

THEIR DRAMATIC STORY. María Victoria was like a walking volcano, words spewing out of her like lava from a live cauldron. Her son Sebas was a perpetual motion machine running excitedly from side to side. What had produced this state of anxiety and restless activity and how did we meet them?

We had set up a charity to work with the many immigrants that were now pouring into Spain, especially those from South America. Clara had brought her friend and distant relative to meet us one day. We were invited to go to a large country 'ranch type' place, tucked away in the Extremadura countryside. Some Colombians from our church had a job there looking after the beautiful old mansion and all the animals. Their own living quarters were very basic but there was even a small private bullring where the owner entertained his upper-class friends from time to time. One or two bulls were slaughtered as the highlight of the day. This was slightly better than some of the Colombians we visited who were looking after pig farms.

Folks were leaving the cars driven by our church members, all eager to spend a relaxing day in the country (a typical church outing in Spain). I suddenly heard the excited babble of a new Colombian lady, short and slim as befitted her recent travels (more to be told of these below). She was accompanied by her four-year-old son. Now, I have been a schoolteacher for most of my life in many different settings and so I can recognise a hyperactive child. It wasn't long before I could see all the symptoms in this poor child Sebas.

He darted from one side to another, fascinated by all there was to see: the sheep, the goats, the oxen and a variety of other animals. It was almost like Noah's Ark. You name an animal, it seemed to be there. His mother tried to keep him with her but got more and more exasperated as the day went on. We heard constant shouts of

'Sebas, come here!'

Sebas seemed to be a little deaf to these cries and therefore we all learnt to help look after Sebas while María Victoria unburdened herself to anyone who would listen.

I found myself on the receiving end of her dramatic story. Being reasonably confident with my Spanish, this lady however was a big challenge to me. No matter how often I asked her to slow down, explaining I was a foreigner in Spain and had never at that stage visited South America, words continued to gush forth. I could see she had come through some deep traumatic events in her life. As we sat there eating our picnic in the lovely spring sunshine we enjoyed in our years in Spain, she continued to talk to me.

With all the violence in Colombia, her brother-in-law had been killed in March 1997 by terrorists. She and her husband didn't really understand why except that he and his family owned land that the terrorists seemed to covet. Then in February 1998 in full daylight they killed her younger brother-in-law right in front of his mother and their family home. As if that wasn't enough, they left threatening notes to say that the father and mother were the next targets followed by María Victoria's husband. In March 1998 the father was killed while having a coffee in the village cafeteria. Three days after the father's funeral, the mother left the village and seven days after that María Victoria's husband decided to leave too. It was the only logical decision left. María Victoria had decided to continue in her work in the village to support herself and Sebas. However she soon was asked by her boss to leave. He simply said

'I am afraid that they will come to kill you here and that would not be good for my business'.

She and her child immediately joined her husband and they began to move from pillar to post around Colombia.

However, each time they began to settle in one town, someone would warn them that they were being watched and off they had to go again. One day her sister rang from France where she was living and said she was going to pull out all the stops to get María Victoria's husband accepted in France as a political refugee. She would also help to pay for her and Sebas to move to Spain to live with her distant relative, Clara, our church member. This all happened according to plan and here we were at the end of April 2001 just after their arrival.

When she stopped to take a breath, I felt I should say something of comfort to this dear lady but what could I say! All my university studies and even my theological training in Denmark had not prepared me for that encounter. All I could share were some incidents from our first years of marriage in Londonderry during the seventies. There we had had our own battles with terrorist organisations. Suddenly I saw a smile on her face. We had bonded. Here was someone who understood her! Much of the details in her story were not grasped that day, I must confess but later I got her to write it down so that I didn't miss much. As I looked at her slim figure and tried to unravel her complicated story, I couldn't help thinking how inappropriate her second name Victoria was, for it of course means 'victory' in English.

However later when we saw her story turn completely around, I was pleased that she had such an appropriate name after all. She was a lady who knew how to battle through life until she came out the other side victorious. Once she had an experience with the living God in our church, she was not afraid to tell others about her new-found faith. We prayed a lot at church for her husband Gustavo and it was a great moment when he was granted permission to join her in Spain. We watched Sebas grow up, eventually able to live without his medication (for hyperactivity). We gave him all the help we could with his studies as he had such difficulty in concentration at school and in church. Desmond learnt to give him little jobs during the service even as a child and he thrived on all the special attention from the pastor.

Gustavo had various health problems. The most serious was cancer and he had to go to Madrid for a course of radiotherapy on his own. At that stage they were living in a tiny one bedroom flat. His instructions were to keep away from his family for 48 hours after finishing the treatment. To our horror we discovered that they were all sleeping in the same bed as soon as he got home. I pointed out how dangerous it was, especially for a young child. They argued how often they had had to live without the father of the house.

'Don't you understand Carolina (as they called me there) how wonderful it is to be together again? Can you blame us for wanting to touch him?'

What more could I say? Absolutely nothing but I did pray a lot and thankfully no harm was done. Some time later, Gustavo was due to return to Madrid for more intensive treatment that was due to last two weeks. The night before he was to leave, a visiting pastor from England approached Desmond.

'I feel a strong urge to pray for that man.'

He knew nothing about his condition but prayed for him. Three days later Gustavo was back home. His wife went into a panic, thinking they had sent him home to die. Far from it; on doing more tests they could find no trace of cancer.

MORE DRAMA. María Victoria's mother was coming over from Colombia and it was a great occasion that they were all waiting for. Suddenly we heard that the mother was not coming after all as she was in prison! Someone had asked to put something in her case and she as an older innocent lady, had agreed. Of course, she never suspected that the package she had, included a quantity of drugs. At the airport the package was opened and she was arrested immediately and thrown into prison. Victoria and all her family spent a lot of money on lawyers to get her out again but she did have to spend several years there.

The last crisis we had with that family involved prison again. Gustavo was driving his scooter to work one day when he met another Colombian woman also on a scooter. He greeted her since he knew her slightly and somehow they had an accident. She tried to blame him for the accident when the police were called to the scene. She was determined to get compensation so she decided to falsely accuse him, even accusing him of sexual assault. He was put into a cell overnight and then was transferred to the local prison for several days. The family were devastated and his work dismissed him immediately when they heard he was in prison. This was a big blow as he had been unemployed for several years and just recently managed to get this new job.

We had constant prayer in the church for him and Sebas, now sixteen, took his place as head of the family. He was a real strength to his mum and constantly assured her that his dad was getting out of prison because he was innocent and we had a just God in charge of the situation. The lady told so many lies that eventually the police realised she had no real case against him and he was released. Rather than take him straight home, they decided to bring him first of all to church. We were in the middle of our mid-week meeting but we decided to stop it there and then. First there was a lot of praise and thanks given to God. Then someone ransacked the church kitchen to find any food we could find and we had a celebration party. Two of Gustavo's sons from another marriage came that night in tears. Though they weren't Christians (both were tough young men in the army) they had to agree that God had certainly answered prayer.

21 PRESSING ON

'Never, never, never, never give up' was a famous saying of Winston Churchill that could equally apply to my husband.

There were often moments of discouragement for me especially but Desmond fortunately had that gift of perseverance. Maybe it came from his love of long distance running which he began as a teenager and still continues.

The South Americans coming to our churches came with all sorts of immoral situations. Once Desmond looked around our congregation and saw only one woman apart from myself that had not had a child out of wedlock. They explained to us that where they lived it was not the custom to get married.

'That is more for the middle classes who can afford a proper wedding', they told us.

Desmond had to preach strong messages on the Biblical view on marriage, fornication and adultery. I found it all quite draining after my strict and rather innocent upbringing to be dealing with these kinds of people all the time. I didn't have a lot in common with our church members to be able to have any of them as real friends at first. Loneliness is a familiar problem among missionaries.

I had a hysterectomy operation which was a little scary. As I was in the recovery room after my operation I seemingly fell out of bed. Too many babies had been born at the same time and the nurse didn't get around to putting up the guards at the sides of my bed. This caused quite a commotion with the surgeon and theatre staff running to put me together again. It could have been dangerous with my drip, my catheter and my previous slipped disc problems. However, I did not suffer any consequences even though the hospital tried to deny that any such incident had actually occurred. They were afraid, I suspect, that we would sue them. We discovered later that our prayer secretary and some ladies were praying at the exact time of my fall and had seen angels around my bed.

EDWIN'S STORY. Another Colombian who came to us in the early days of our time in Badajoz was Edwin. Edwin was a tall burly young man from a whole family of professional criminals in Bogotá. His appearance was enough to ward off anyone who tried to go against him. He had spent a year in Germany as a political refugee and had got into crime. To run away from the police, he decided to come to Spain on a short visit. He met Oscar who soon invited him to live in his flat and shared the gospel. I remember the night he was converted. Anna Pienaar, a student helper, was preaching for the first time ever and, as a 21 year old, was very nervous. Much to her delight, Edwin responded.

A former girlfriend followed him from Germany and she too was converted. They married and she became pregnant. However, Edwin was in the country illegally and the police finally caught up with him the day before his first child was born. Desmond went to the police station to try to speak for him, to plead how he was reformed and so forth, but was not even allowed to speak to him. His wife was devastated and we shared in the pain of the moment. After a few years, Edwin suddenly appeared and we wondered how. He was reluctant to tell us the truth that he had in fact come back under a false passport. He was envious of the other Colombians who had stayed in our church. Edwin could see that they had grown so much spiritually in the years he was away. He was in and out of the church as his old lifestyle with drugs was still pulling him back. Another child was born and this time we managed to dedicate the baby and have a lovely family celebration with them. The very next day Edwin was arrested and deported. His wife and family stayed in Spain for some years but recently decided to go back to Colombia where they could be a family again. They contact us from time to time on Facebook. They always thank us for being parents and bringing them into a relationship with God.

TANIA'S STORY. A Bolivian lady, recently widowed, arrived in the church one morning with her three children. Tania was very attractive and as often happens, began to live with a Spaniard. The Latin American ladies are often attracted to Spanish men, believing that to be their answer if they have left a poor country.

The Spaniard in this case was divorced and in the military. She brought him to church and he was very soon converted and they eventually married.

There began a process of uniting two lots of children, the Bolivians and the Spaniards, and there was often conflict. They were very grateful for the marriage courses we were able to run in the church. We were often called out to their flat to sort out a conflict as we were at the beginning with Enrique and Luz Denia. They had gone through an even more difficult situation as the two lots of children were living with them. In these times of crisis, we felt so weak and lacking in wisdom but the Holy Spirit as always was there and brought harmony once more.

OUR INTERNATIONAL CHURCH CONTINUES. The Latin Americans continued to come, representing most of the countries of that area and they brought with them much fervour to our church. So we soon became quite an international and multicultural gathering, very different from our earlier Spanish only churches. They loved to all pray aloud at the same time, something very new for us in the west. All-night prayer meetings were a struggle for us British but they loved them. They believed the church was going to grow. This was a change from the Spaniards who were always so quick to talk about how hard it was in Spain to build churches. They had no difficulty believing in the supernatural and some possibly saw more answers to prayers for healing than we did ourselves.

One Spanish lady who was converted at that time got very frustrated that she had no Spanish ladies of her age in the church to befriend her. She could not understand why so many Protestant churches in Spain are full of Latin American immigrants. This caused her to speak to Gabino Fernández, the historian and evangelical writer, who had come to preach one Sunday. Here was his reply.

'We Spaniards are quite racist and God is allowing this to teach us to relate to one another in Kingdom fashion. It is very humbling for us Spaniards to find God using foreigners to reach our own people'.

151

They had little money themselves but were always keen to make money for the church. We began to have a sample of Latin American cooking done by someone before our Sunday morning service. This was then sold after the meeting. To us the food was not all that different, whether it was from Colombia, Bolivia, Ecuador, Uruguay, Brazil or wherever but to them of course it was vastly different. It was very important that the pastor and his wife sample everything and approve and we often went home with no appetite for a normal Sunday lunch.

Quite a few joined the Spanish army and when they went abroad on service we were sometimes invited to the ceremony at the barracks and treated royally.

Not all were success stories. A Brazilian girl came who was a pastor's daughter. She told me how her mother had been so intent on church work that according to her, she was neglected.

Another pastor's son from Angola arrived one Sunday and wanted to come in with his dog. He was obviously under the influence of drugs. Desmond was away on that occasion and Oscar was preaching. When we refused to let him in with the dog, he caused quite a commotion and no one could listen to Oscar's message.

'Doesn't God love animals?' he shouted.

Oscar wisely addressed him publicly and said he could bring in his dog. This he did and I accompanied them in the front row to make sure there was no more commotion. He came several times without his dog, I should add, and we did all we could but neither the Brazilian girl nor he came back to God. We were always so sad when this sort of thing happened and how sad their parents must be too.

When the Presbyterian church closed down we inherited their two Spanish members. One was an alcoholic and a real embarrassment to us at first. He was proud of the fact that his parents had been some of the first Protestants in Badajoz and had suffered a lot for their faith. Due to alcohol however, he had lost his wife, his daughter and his hairdressing business. A few times we had to stop him coming into the service as he was slightly tipsy or he would want to come right in with a cigarette still in his mouth. Since Desmond was leading or preaching, it usually fell to me to refuse him entry. Eventually he was freed from alcohol and we all rejoiced. He brought other alcoholics to our services too. However, his health, both physical and mental, had been ruined by the alcohol and he died in middle age.

As often happens in times of discouragement, God has his own way of encouraging us. We were invited to a sales event when the organiser suddenly approached us saying

'Ramón, you are my spiritual father!'

We discovered that Miguel Angel Pino had been in our church in Córdoba when he was fourteen. He even remembered the Bible verse Desmond had preached on that night when he came to faith. We had lost contact with him but he was now a Baptist pastor in Seville as well as a salesman. It was a lovely surprise when he immediately arranged for us to speak in his church. Miguel Angel was an accomplished musician and he reminded me how I had encouraged him to write songs. He had just returned from the USA where he had listened to one of his songs that had been translated into English in a Vineyard church.

On another occasion Desmond had taken two of our young folk to the Córdoba youth camp. This had become one of the biggest youth camps in the country and folk came from all over. Again, a middle-aged man approached him with the same comment. He had come to faith with us many years before in Andújar, had gone away from God for many years, but was now back living in Córdoba. He reminded Desmond

'Don't you remember praying and God healed me?'

THE ECUADORIANS. We had folk from Ecuador but the most interesting group were the Chango family, indigenous Indians from the mountains near Ambato. They kept together a lot as a family and took years to really mix and become friends with the rest of the members in the church. Finally, they did after aunts, uncles and cousins arrived. They were so intent on sending back money to the poor folk in their village where there was no running water or electricity. They still have lots of projects to assist with. This is very commendable as some immigrants are so overcome by the wealth in Europe that they are only interested in working to keep buying material things for themselves. This family love to perform their colourful native dances which they have done for us at several church events. At our farewell they dressed up in their native costumes and presented us with one each. I was given the typical frilly white blouse with embroidered flowers and Desmond a red cloak. We then had to put them on and wear them for the rest of the evening.

PERUVIANS. We were blessed with Peruvians, including a dentist in our congregation for some years. Not only did he give us good discounts for our treatment but he even brought his instruments to church on two occasions. There he finished the treatment in our church kitchen after the service!

A SPECIAL WEDDING AND THE FAMILY THAT FOLLOWED. Our son Michael was very independent by this stage, having qualified as a BA pilot. We were delighted when he introduced us to his girlfriend Kathryn, an air hostess from Lisburn in Northern Ireland. In June 2003 they were married in the same Presbyterian church there as my brother had been many years before. It was a wonderful day. I had often worried about how we would eventually organise a wedding for Michael with us living in Spain but once again my God had it all under control. The bride's family did most of the organising and got to know my sister and her husband who lived nearby them. We along with the groom's party stayed with my sister and their beautiful garden was ideal for wedding photos.

Twelve pilots were guests as well as ten airhostesses from British Airways and all the good BA training came out on the day. I had so many of them ask if I was comfortable and enjoying the day. It almost felt like being on a long-haul flight without the jet lag! One very glamorous air hostess remarked,

'I have been watching you all day and you have been so peaceful and composed. You haven't cried as most mothers do when their sons get married.'

She asked me to explain this. Needless to say, I was able to explain how God had changed me from being a very tearful and fearful person. She then agreed to my suggestion to go on an Alpha course. I was particularly happy on that day to know that our one and only son now had someone close to look after him.

Eventually their son Harry was born in May 2006. Michael wanted to make sure we didn't miss out at the birth so he made his own video of the event. I was so excited that day in my English classes. Someone even wrote a poem for me in English imagining how I must feel with the birth of my first grandchild. In every class I somehow managed to teach and discuss the birth. On the second day after the birth we had a phone call to say that Michael was speaking Spanish to his son and to check that it wasn't too soon. I encouraged him that that was great. Harry was able to speak a little and understand when he came to visit us in Badajoz. He was a big attraction both in our church and with our neighbours. Unfortunately, Michael was not able to keep up the Spanish when the two other children arrived. It does require a lot of discipline when only one of the parents speak a second language. Sophie was born in November 2008 and another boy Robbie in September 2010. I found it heart-breaking not to be closer at these times to enjoy my grandchildren.

TRAINING OF CHURCH LEADERS. Meanwhile we trained leaders, thanks to help from our church in Basingstoke. Oscar also spent nine months training with Pastor Daniel Chamorro and his group of leaders in Gandia, Valencia. We had to watch them make mistakes but God honoured them and many more were brought into the church and transformed by a relationship with God. Numbers grew to about a hundred at our Sunday meetings. With enthusiastic leaders keen to evangelise we were able to begin an outreach in two nearby villages – Corte de Pelea and La Roca de la Sierra.

A NEW CHURCH PLANT. A Brazilian family had arrived in La Roca and were fervently praying for a church to be established. Cristina the mother was the first to arrive. She was then followed by a son and daughter who were Christians. Cristina had had a very hard life with several children by different fathers. In a very dubious club in Extremadura she had met an elderly Spaniard who fell in love with her and asked her to live with him in the village. What he didn't realise was that she was going to turn his life upside down. He was practically an alcoholic. Her children led her to the Lord and she then wanted to have meetings in her house but he was very opposed. The first time Desmond went to his door, he screamed at him and refused to let him in. It was wonderful to watch how she gained him through her love over the years and they actually got married in our Badajoz church just after we left Spain. Oscar now married with his wife Paola, was the main evangelist in La Roca along with us. We enjoyed being pioneers again and going into new territory.

CATHOLIC CONFERENCE ON FAMILY. By this time, we were quite well known in the city of Badajoz. Desmond had quite a few radio and TV interviews especially on the Catholic channel. In 2008 we were invited to a Catholic conference on family for the region of Extremadura. As Desmond was unable to attend, I was on my own but got a special welcome from the platform as the wife of the 'British Protestant pastor from Badajoz whom everybody knows!' There were five hundred delegates there, all involved in some sort of ministry in their local Catholic church to strengthen the family. Some of those giving seminars were very keen to know what we Protestants were doing about marriage courses, abortion, homosexuality and in vitro insemination. At times I was able to put them in touch with someone working in that area. On the whole I saw that they were doing a lot to strengthen the family in each local parish, even in the villages and this had to be admired. The population of Spain is 46.5 million. Most are Catholics in name at least and only 1.5 million are evangelical Christians.

HOME, SWEET HOME – NOT ALWAYS SO SWEET! In every home where we lived in Badajoz, we had some sort of crisis. In the first flat someone tampered with our lock and damaged the wood all around it. They had obviously tried to get in though the neighbours couldn't believe it. They assured me that there had never been any robberies in our block. We were very conscious that someone was trying to disturb us. In the next flat a neighbour had a young wife on drugs. She used to arrive home very late at night. When the husband refused to let her in, the entire block of flats and those in the area were all awakened by her pleadings,

'Let me in, let me in!'

This led to a court case by the neighbours and eventually they left much to our relief but not before we had lost many nights of sleep.

In our final home in what we believed was a quiet and rather select area of the city we had neighbours with a difficult teenager. In fact, once she along with her gang of friends stole our solar lights from the small garden we had and I watched it all from our bedroom window. The parents decided to buy her a drum kit and where did they decide to install it? In their lounge! We spoke to them about the noise since the walls between the two houses were so thin. On occasions we could even hear their arguments in our bedroom when one or other of them arrived home a little tipsy at 3 am. Their answer was simply

'We didn't install it upstairs to disturb you in your bedroom nor downstairs in the basement to disturb your English classes'.

They were convinced they had made the best decision. We persevered and when the drumming began in the middle of our pupils' Cambridge exams, that was the limit of our patience.

Some of my adult pupils had told me how to complain again to them about the noise factor, well beyond the legal limit for Spain. The wife just exploded in true Spanish style. Why had we ever come to live next door to them with all our British customs so different to theirs? We got up early on a Sunday morning while they wanted to sleep! We went to bed early when they wanted to have parties! Why couldn't we look for a house elsewhere? So, the list went on. Fortunately, God had been teaching me about not being easily offended so I was able to throw my arm around her and wait until her anger abated. The next day she came to apologise, saying

'I know God has sent you here to bring peace and harmony in our road'.

In fact, later we became good friends. Her daughter got into trouble with the police because of her violence and was sent to a home for young offenders. Before that I was asked to invite her in and give her little jobs as the parents thought that I was the only one who could really understand her! I alone among the neighbours was allowed to know about her whereabouts as the parents were so ashamed of course. I encouraged our young people's group to write letters to her and she wrote some very emotional replies, thanking them for being real friends. She committed her life to God and came to church a few times but later began to study and settle down and we lost touch.

Desmond had on several occasions brought some peace into the very heated arguments that can arise in the community meetings run by the neighbours' association. Once the neighbours had objected to some dangerous dogs kept under very unhygienic conditions in a garden in our road. The owners refused to do anything so suddenly the dogs were poisoned. It was obviously by one of our neighbours and the police came to interview us all but the culprit was never found. On another occasion, a lady objected to the leaves that were falling onto their lawn from a neighbour's tree. These neighbours, a psychiatrist and medical consultant came home after a week-end away to find their garden all withered and burnt up. Someone had sprayed it with weed killer. You can see there was never a dull moment for us wherever we decided to live in Spain.

22 WE'RE IN THIS TOGETHER

You never know what you'll get into if you follow God. Here we were in Extremadura, the poorest area of Spain and one of the least evangelised. One of its strengths was the region's *Council of Evangelical Churches* that was formed just after we arrived there. Each church was represented at a three monthly meeting. Most of the churches were small and few and far between, so we realised that together we could achieve more. My husband became the treasurer of the group and ended up teaching a lot of the Spanish and South American pastors how to keep accounts. They simply didn't see the need to do so.

'Why do we have to give account for any money that comes through our hands? Can't the people trust us?' they said to us.

Desmond had learnt the Spanish system of accounting from one of the three couples we befriended right at the beginning in Badajoz. He was an accountant in a local bank and was therefore able to help us to wade through the complicated accounting and tax systems. The Evangelical Council had to keep proper accounts and pastors had to learn when the government began to give out grants to help integrate the immigrants.

Desmond was one of the first to realise how we could use these to our advantage. He applied for a grant for Enrique who then gave up his job to work for the church full time. To make up his salary the church also supported him with a small sum each month. We had realised people needed to learn to support a pastor and not just depend on foreigners paid from abroad or working as tentmakers like ourselves. Together we opened a second hand clothes corner at the back of the church building. Many of my new middle-class friends were happy to donate clothes.

KLESIS AND SOCIAL ACTION. President of Klesis sounds impressive, doesn't it? That was Desmond's new title. Klesis was a dying entity set up by some Protestants in Badajoz as a social action arm of the church and he had been asked to breathe new life into it. It was eventually incorporated into the Evangelical council and became the social action arm of all the churches in Extremadura so all could benefit. Food was received from the Red Cross. The churches then distributed it to any needy people who registered. In that way the churches served their local communities. Later a government body provided food. At first, we found that immigrants were going from our church to other Catholic churches; in other words to get food from several places of distribution. Soon Enrique learnt to have detailed forms to give out to each family to ensure that they only received food in one place. When the economic crisis came we found ourselves providing food for needy Spanish families as well as immigrant ones.

Later the North Africans arrived in the city and we were inundated by Muslim women looking for clothes and food. However we had to be careful as we discovered some were taking the clothes off to Morocco and selling them there. Enrique became an adviser for many sad and needy immigrants that came into the church building during the week. A number of these were prayed for and given literature. I too had my first experience of praying in French for Muslims who came in looking for help. Sometimes they could only speak French or Arabic and we had tracts, DVDs and copies of the Bible to give them in those languages. I still remember one political refugee from Syria weep when I gave him a Bible.

'I have studied the Koran a lot but have so longed to have a Bible to read' he told me amidst the sobs.

Many seeds were sown and only eternity will tell the fruitfulness of that ministry.

BIBLE EXHIBITIONS AND CELEBRATIONS. If President of Klesis wasn't enough, try this for size; 'Councillor for Education and Culture of the Evangelical Council of Extremadura'. That was Desmond's new post for some years.

In February 2002 he organised a Bible exhibition in the main Exhibition Hall in Badajoz. It was a five day event to commemorate the fourth centenary of the publication of the Bible most used in Protestant churches in the whole Spanish speaking world. Many different versions and translations were on display, including a New Testament in the almost extinct Extremaduran language. The first Bible translated into Spanish was particularly popular as it was the work of a monk from Extremadura named Casiodoro de Reina in 1569. He was considered a heretic for making the Bible available to the public and had to flee from the country. Another monk from the same area, Cipriano de Valera had to flee as well. In 1602 he published a revised version of the 1569 edition. While both lived in other parts of Europe their effigies were burnt in Seville by the Spanish Inquisition. Both versions became forbidden books by the Catholic Church in Spain until 1948. Desmond translated into Spanish the unedited letter written in Badajoz by George Borrow, the first Bible colporteur sent by the British and Foreign Bible Society to Spain. This exhibition was well received both by the public and the media. The visit of the Catholic Archbishop was a significant event in the full programme. The exhibition then became a travelling one being replicated on a smaller scale in seven other towns and cities in the region.

On another occasion we celebrated the arrival in Spain in 1834 of George Borrow. What's the big deal? Well, from the 16th century Reformation until the early 19th century Spain had been closed to any attempt to introduce the gospel as we know it today. Catholicism in Spain in the 19th century was largely socially retrograde, superstitious and ignorant. Colporteurs were basically travelling Bible salesmen seeking to introduce people to the reading and studying of the Scriptures. This was one of the most effective ways the gospel message had of opening minds. The year 1834 is often referred to as the start of the Second Reformation in Spain. George Borrow was one of the foremost figures in this movement. He crossed the Spanish border from Portugal at Badajoz and stayed several weeks in the city. His time was mostly spent speaking to the Gypsy people. It was in Badajoz he began translating the New Testament into their language, 'Calao'.

To celebrate this the Evangelical Council organised a day's trip called 'In the Steps of George Borrow'. The bus load of people gathered around Gabino Fernández Campos, a Protestant historian and guide for the day. What were two Gypsy pastors doing there? Nothing more and nothing less than to receive a copy of the translation of the New Testament from the hand of the great man himself. That was Desmond dressed as a 19th century gentlemen. After a short speech 'Borrow' presented the New Testament to the Gypsy pastors. One of them read the parable of the Prodigal Son, a text Borrow had used a lot when visiting the gypsies more than a century and a half earlier! A truly memorable celebration organized by Desmond in his role as Education and Culture Councillor. The mayor also sent a representative to the ceremony. The Bible society organised a special conference at another date and Desmond was one of the speakers on the life of George Borrow.

WRITERS' EVENTS. I organised with my husband several Writers' Days. I never considered myself a writer but on the mission field as a pioneer you learn to be a 'Jack of all trades'. In September 2003 I had attended a four day Seminar in Madrid run by the Latin American Association of Christian Writers which was helpful when I was still trying to publish my first book in Spanish. That experience then gave me more confidence to help others with their writing and also put me in touch with other Spaniards who came to speak at our writers' days. For many years Enrique was inspired to be the editor of a magazine done in newspaper style for all the churches in Extremadura.

It was the annual book fair, an important part of life in Spain. I was manning the stall for the evangelical churches in Badajoz. The first minister of the Extremadura Parliament was visiting the stalls accompanied by the city mayor.

'How is your son? Is he still a pilot with BA?' asked the first minister.

The mayor was perplexed! *Whoever was this English lady the first minister just greeted in such warm personal terms?* We had given English lessons to his son some years before. This helped give credibility to this church initiative.

The book fair is where the middle class especially go to listen to talks by famous writers. They will buy books at the many bookstalls and have them signed in a special tent. Then the pastors decided that since I was the only one among them who had published a book, I should ask for a place in the 'tent for signing'. It was a battle royal with the authorities but I was finally given a place among these famous authors. I was rather nervous. This was an even bigger challenge than my hour-long interview on a Madrid Christian radio station about my book some time before. That interview had been at 1 am after a hot summer's day. I had great difficulty keeping awake before the interview began but I was assured that that was a favourite hour for the Spaniards to listen to the radio!

On this occasion I was hobnobbing with a group of well-known authors. Some had been travelling all around Europe visiting book fairs and it was my very first time. The churches were told to come and visit me so that I would not feel the 'poor relation' among all these more popular authors. The conversation among us all was very interesting and I was able to share a little about my faith with some of these authors. Each of us had to share why we had written our book and something about it.

The Minister for Culture asked me what I was writing at present and I told her I was compiling a book of children's stories. In fact, I had only written one of the stories. The others were written by Christian ladies from the area. She encouraged me to put it in for the competition they were holding. I enjoyed my few hours of fame, as you can imagine, and I went home and laughed and laughed. 1 Corinthians 1:27 came to mind for 'God has chosen the foolish things of the world to confound the wise; and God has chosen the weak things of the world to confound the things which are mighty.'

A GOSPEL CHOIR. A gospel choir in Spain singing pieces in English. What's this all about? I was part of this gospel choir in Extremadura that sang some pieces in English. It was organised for all the churches combined. One of my roles, when we made a DVD with other gospel choirs from all over the country, was to correct the English pronunciation for the English songs. There was usually a good spirit of unity among the churches in Extremadura perhaps because we were all small and realised that we needed each other. This was not always so in other parts of Spain. We made many good friends with other missionaries from the UK,

France, Germany, the Netherlands, Luxembourg, Switzerland, Norway, Sweden, Finland, Canada, USA and of course Latin America. Each September everyone looked forward to the special church day when all the churches met together in a big open air park in Plasencia. Some had to travel as much as 200 km. Extremadura is a big place, roughly the size of Wales.

RETREATS AND LADIES' DAYS. Can't you just imagine it, a crowd of ladies on a retreat, one outside toilet? Don't you just love running the gauntlet of the rats just to go to the loo in the middle of the night? I was so angry when I found myself making my way by torchlight to the toilet along a slippery wet path. It was at the retreat for pastors' wives and missionaries held every two years. I remember feeling angry because I had just returned from a conference for church leaders in England in a Marriott hotel! That had seemed just too luxurious for me and even then, some leaders had complained about the food. Now it seemed to me unfair that Spaniards had to have a retreat in such conditions. This was the first retreat that I attended held in a small Christian camp centre. I remember we found everything so dirty that we had to wash all the plates and cutlery before beginning to do our own cooking. I was disappointed that I could not raise finance from our home churches for future retreats. Fortunately, we did find better places in future years. Some American missionaries got funding once from their church to allow us to be in a three-star hotel. The last retreats that I attended were memorable too. I had to both speak and be a counsellor for the other ladies. This we realised was important as there was always someone arriving with serious issues to sort out. On several occasions I wrote dramas that were performed at these retreats. This was a very liberating experience for me as my father had not allowed me to be in school dramas even though I was commended for my acting ability. He believed that all acting was sinful.

Think about it: 170 women packed into a hall with comfortable seating for 120. Yes, it was the annual day conference for the ladies of the churches of Extremadura. This rotated around the churches and in October 2008 it was our turn to host it in our church building. To make matters worse we had to provide a hot meal for them! It was a major undertaking for our church to provide breakfast, lunch and coffee and cakes for 170 ladies who arrived as well as organising the main morning meeting and afternoon workshops. All the skills of the Latin Americans were used to teach crafts, jewellery making and beauty workshops. The following year we all realised the conference had to be in a bigger public hall. A church football league was also formed and our church team proudly wore their own special uniform, winning the league in their first year.

CHALLENGE OF RADIO AND TV. Have you ever imagined you would be speaking on radio and TV? I certainly didn't. The idea terrified me but I was particularly grateful to be able to take part in various training days for speaking on the radio. There we were able to make our own programme and receive constructive criticism from experienced folk who worked in the media. I had refused to go on radio or TV before that each time I was invited. However, these days gave me a lot more confidence and I was amazed at the grace God then gave me to speak on radio and TV.

It was our last annual Churches' Day out before we returned to the UK and we were rewarded at our farewell with two lovely plaques to thank us for our service. This was a great honour which I knew my husband well deserved as he had put a lot of work into the council of churches.

23 LATIN AMERICA. HERE WE COME!

ARGENTINA. My childhood dreams were coming true and I was finally visiting these countries I had heard about as a child and seen in all those missionary slides. The views from the window of the aeroplane were spectacular as we watched dawn break over the Andes. I could hardly believe I was actually in Argentina. How did these visits come about?

In 2001 Desmond had had the privilege of going to Buenos Aires, Argentina to interpret for a group of English pastors. They went to observe a revival that was taking place in the church of Claudio and Betty Freidzon. They also visited a top security prison where the Holy Spirit was moving. He came back so impressed that he wanted to take me to see the revival in Argentina for myself. This we were able to do at the invitation of Pastor Daniel Chamorro, a renewed Baptist Pastor. We went to his main church in Plottier in Patagonia and it was such an encouragement. As Desmond often says, he preached the same sermons as in Badajoz, but there was power in the meetings and folk were healed and set free.

It was a real treat to speak to 80 young people from Baptist churches in the region about trans-cultural mission. They had chosen this from other seminars because they believed they had a call and wanted to hear from us older folk. We were asked to speak for an hour and a half and I remember thinking aloud, as a past teacher of teenagers, *We will be sure to lose their attention long before the end*. It was quite the contrary. They listened spellbound and even queued up to ask us questions afterwards, especially those who believed they were called to Spain. They weren't used to all the gimmicks we sometimes have to use here in the West to keep them in the church and still have a great respect for the older generation.

On that trip I was amazed at the number of Christian books available that I couldn't buy in Spain. Argentina had been a hard field for British missionaries many years ago but after revival, churches had grown and were making an impact on their cities.

HONDURAS. Can you imagine me walking around the city under a beautiful white lacy parasol and being stared at by the natives? I was now in San Pedro Sula, Honduras. When Desmond was working with the Chamber of Commerce he was invited by a rather upper-class Spaniard to speak at the Chamber of Commerce in that city. With our son now being a pilot with British Airways we were able to get good discounts on long haul flights so we enjoyed quite a few trips for some years. We were not able to visit any churches there on that short visit but we did notice how many there were and how active they were. We had spoken to a girl on the plane and her mother was coming to meet her at the airport. The mother immediately sensed that we were Christians and asked if no one had come to meet us at the airport. Having flown by standby and thus missing several flights, our business colleague had not turned up. She immediately insisted on getting a taxi for us and agreeing the proper fare with him before leaving us. She didn't want us to be charged an enormous fare as can often happen with us British in a foreign country.

While Desmond was at the conference I was taken around the city by the man's wife under her very posh parasol. A few times folk came out on the streets to evangelise. I was keen to talk but the lady kept rushing me past them, saying

'These are sects. Don't you realise?'

On one occasion she couldn't remember where she had parked her car. We were there looking everywhere for it when a group from a church building came out to ask if they could help her. She reluctantly told them her dilemma and in no time at all they had found the car for us. However, she was still convinced they were a sect no matter how I tried to educate her that there were other valid Christian churches as well as the Catholic one she knew.

When leaving the country, I had another interesting experience. Since we were on standby and thus the last to enter the plane, we were told at the door that only one could travel and with no luggage. The pilot had decided that there was too much weight on the plane! It was a shock and Desmond kindly let me choose whether I would stay alone in Honduras or travel on to Miami. Without hesitation I decided Miami as I had seen enough guns and guards everywhere in Honduras. He pushed some dollars into my hand and I got into the plane in a rather dazed state, having left all my luggage with him. Imagine my surprise to notice that my fellow traveller in the plane was reading a large Bible, so before long I shared my story with her. She was quick to pray and fill me with faith.

'You will see how God will look after you in Miami' were her words to me in Spanish. He certainly did.

I suddenly remembered that we had had an older lady from Miami to help us for three months at the beginning of our time in Badajoz. We had lost contact with her but I still had her telephone number and address in my little address book. I rang her and discovered that Desmond had already had the same idea and she was about to get into her car and come to collect me at the airport. It was such an answer to prayer and she took me first to show me the famous Miami beaches. Then at her home, she gave me a toothbrush, nightdress and a comfortable bed. We did not have mobile phones then so Desmond and I had no way to communicate but she had got from him the number of the hotel where he was spending the night. He was then able to tell us which flight he was getting the next day. Once again God was looking after us in spite of all my initial anxiety.

BOLIVIA. Imagine us trying to cross a river near Baures on the north-eastern side of Bolivia near Brazil. To our horror we discovered that our vehicle had to negotiate some old planks before getting onto a rickety boat that would hopefully get us to the other side of the river. *Would we ever make it?* was our thought once again but we didn't dare express such doubt in the transport system of the country we were visiting. Moreover, Desmond was driving.

A couple from Bolivia called Erica and Hugo had become very special to us when in Badajoz. Erica was a primary school teacher but her qualifications were not accepted in Spain so she had to take a simple cleaning job like many professional people who came. After a few years they felt they had to go back to their homeland to look after elderly parents and help revive a church that was struggling. However, they wanted us to still remain as their pastor and visit them whenever possible. This I did three times and Desmond four.

Our first trip was 2005. We flew to Santa Cruz, then in a smaller plane to Trinidad and finally a very small single-engine one to Baures on the edge of the jungle. In fact this plane had no seats and I was told,

'You may sit on your suitcase but the men have to sit on the floor'.

There were just five of us in the plane, including a pastor who sat beside the pilot since he was the heaviest passenger. Imagine our surprise when the pastor began to pilot the plane. I asked if he had a licence to do this and was greeted with bursts of laughter from the three Bolivians.

'Who needs a licence? In this country' they replied, 'lots of people are driving cars without a licence!'

Before getting into this plane in Trinidad our friends had arranged for us to spend time with their cousin who was an air traffic controller. This had not filled us with confidence about flying in Bolivia as he told us how they managed without radar! I was wondering again would we ever make it. I can honestly say I never get nervous in planes but this time I did. The noise inside the small aircraft was deafening and the view beneath us was the Amazon jungle. I began to prepare myself to meet my Maker and spent most of the journey singing worship songs aloud. It was a relief when we actually landed in the large field that was Baures' airfield. The one room terminal building looked pathetic to western eyes but they were so proud of it as an Australian missionary had built it.

My first impressions of Baures with its thatched houses seemed more like an African village. The poverty of Bolivia was tremendous and made a lasting impression on me. We were staying in one of the most expensive houses in the village yet they had only the very basic furniture, a table and beds. There were no arm chairs and definitely no ornaments. We had to learn to relax on a hammock when the mosquitoes left us alone. The kitchen and toilet were outside of the main house where we could have a cold shower each morning; no such luxury as hot water.

Yet the generosity of the people again was unbelievable. They decided to kill the fatted calf for us and on two occasions at 5 am we were rudely awakened by the killing outside our bedroom window. The meat was then put into their freezer which they were proud of, to be given to us a few days later. These were educated people but completely unperturbed by the fact that the freezer was constantly on and off. The village only had electricity for a few hours each day. Baures does not receive many tourists so we were soon taken to see the mayor and the new priest who was German. With tears in his eyes he told us how he was struggling to settle in and appreciated the fact that we understood. I again thanked God that He had called me to live in Spain which was a lot easier than Latin America.

We had to eat simply what was in season. I had so much yucca cooked in many different ways that I never wanted to see a yucca in my life again. The villagers invited us to their humble homes for a meal and hygiene was not great but we were amazed that we never had any stomach sicknesses. As the old country preacher said

'Where He leads me I will follow; what he feeds me, I will swallow.'

Perhaps that was because a lot of folk in the UK and Spain were praying for us. It certainly stretched us to get up in time to speak at a 6.30 am meeting. People had walked for miles to get there and others arrived in open-backed lorries where they were packed in like sardines. We also went to help evangelise in some of the nearby villages which were very poor.

British missionaries are welcomed in style in Bolivia. They were so pleased to show us church buildings built by missionaries and a hospital that had been built by an Australian one. I looked at the dirty concrete floors and the extremely basic facilities and struggled to find words to admire it as they obviously expected.

Desmond often says that no one would think of him as an evangelist for a campaign in a football stadium, but in Baures he found himself in that position. The stadium was full and God moved. Over 50 people responded to the invitation to accept Christ. On another occasion in Trinidad he was asked to preach in an Assemblies of God church where the pastor was the president of that denomination. In each place we met pastors who were burnt out and asked us for help with finance. We were able to help some but how we would have loved to have more to share with them and their families.

One year someone tried to arrange a meeting between us and the president Evo Morales. We had collected some money towards a proposed Christian school and seemingly Evo is keen to meet foreigners who bring finance into the country. A visit to La Paz was arranged but we became quite weak with altitude sickness and would have been unable to see him even if the visit had come off. I found myself on the plane beside a high-up government official and had a very interesting conversation. I had been prepared for this conversation by a prophecy given to me some months before in a conference in Madrid. A German lady pastor working with Rheinhard Bonnke had told me ,

'Be bold and not afraid when you are brought before government officials!'

How did we ever collect money in Spain for a school in Bolivia? Our church was very generous in their giving but I knew I had to find some other solution. One day after praying about it, I heard two elderly German ladies speaking in a local supermarket. I distinctly heard God say,

'Go and speak to them and they will help with the finance'.

In obedience I did and discovered they had recently come to live in the area. To my surprise they invited me to visit them. I then discovered that one of them was quite a famous artist. When I finally plucked up courage to ask her to help with finance for Bolivia, her immediate response was,

'I'd be delighted to do so'.

We were given a generous gift from the sale of her pictures and even a beautiful one for me to keep!

Our last trip to Bolivia was very memorable for two reasons. We were robbed and though we raced back to our hotel to report the losses and ring our bank, about £700 was already taken out of our bank account in the UK. We told no-one but obviously prayed a lot. Within less than a month we had been sent money by various folk. The money amounted to exactly £700.

The second incident was at the airport as we prepared to leave. Because we were travelling on a standby ticket, we were the last to enter the aircraft. This meant we got very close to Evo Morales who was welcoming his great friend Hugo Chávez, the then president of Venezuela. There was a lot of pomp and ceremony as the two men met and I began to shudder. I believe I was sensing the evil presence and darkness that surrounds those two men. It certainly made me pray more fervently for those two countries.

Though we never got to Cuba, I once met a Cuban psychiatrist in Spain and was able to testify a little. He mentioned that he was alone in Spain without his wife and children and could not return to Cuba. Without hesitation I found myself talking about how, as a result of prayer in our church, we had seen many families re-united. I promised to pray for his case. He listened carefully and though I never saw him again, I did hear from a psychologist to whom I gave English lessons. She told me that his family had miraculously managed to get out of Cuba and they were a happy family once more.

Those experiences and our trips to Latin America made a big impact on us as well as the gypsies mentioned in the next chapter.

24 THE GYPSY MOVEMENT

TEACHING LUIS. I can still remember his large brown eyes and dark sallow skin, his features which make the gypsies stand out from other Spaniards. This was Luis who was to become a great friend for our son.

Michael suddenly said one day,

'I would really like to have another boy in my home-school class.'

So we prayed together for that. The other pupil arrived most unexpectedly. A gypsy pastor and his family began to attend our services. He was having a year out from pastoring and preaching as he was having trouble with his voice. He happened to remark how his son Luis was so struggling in school and could neither read nor write. Classes usually had forty pupils or more so the teacher couldn't give special attention to anyone who was struggling. In fact, they often ignored the gypsy children who were usually rather unruly and had a bad reputation in any case.

Since Luis was seven, the same age as Michael, we decided to invite him to join our class in the afternoon. The tuition was then in Spanish. He told us on the first day,

'I need to read so that I can read and teach the Bible like my Dad. I need to learn to count to be able to sell in the market.'

This was what most gypsies did so we all three prayed for that. Michael read aloud to him some nature books we had and his eyes got bigger and bigger with delight.

'I never heard these things before,' he would tell us.

We had been to his home and saw how he simply slept on a mattress on the floor with no toys at all. This was a great opportunity to teach Michael to share his toys and treat with respect those less fortunate than himself.

We discovered he was very good at football and Michael had less experience in that area so we gave him lots of praise for that. He very quickly learned to read, write and do his sums so we all were delighted that God had answered our prayers. After the class he could stay around and play with all of Michael's toys which he treated so carefully. A year later the family moved on to another town but they came back to visit us once and to thank us. They were so excited that Luis' teacher in his new school had gone to a meeting at their gypsy church. She had been so impressed with Luis' work and behaviour in school that she wanted to learn more about the family.

GYPSY MEETINGS. The real gypsies in Spain are not itinerant but live in houses usually in the poorest areas of the town. Some say they originated in India. From the beginning of our time in Spain we enjoyed going to a gypsy church service. While their worship and preaching was very loud and we couldn't easily make out the words, we could always sense the presence of God in the meetings. It was a real 'pick me up' for us both. These are the real gypsies.

Until the massive influx of Latin American immigrants, the gypsy movement accounted for the majority of evangelical believers in Spain. It began fifty years ago out of revival and they still see lots of miracles among them. They are present in most cities and towns, with over 1,400 churches, and are known as the *Halleluiah* people. Officially their churches are called *Philadelphia* and are strongly Pentecostal and very loud.

I have already mentioned the gypsy contacts in Córdoba. In Badajoz however, we had a lot more contact with their pastors, especially Fernando Navarro and his wife. Fernando had built up a very successful drug rehabilitation centre in the city which was well recognised by the town council. Out of that one of the largest of their churches in the city was founded. He also pioneered a radio station where Desmond and other·pastors spoke from time to time. I too had a one hour live interview on another occasion. They were always keen for me to run a programme from our church each week. By this time I had lost my fear of the media and would have loved to do that. As often happens, there was just not enough time, especially since we were both working to support ourselves.

Fernando was one of the national leaders of the movement and responsible for training pastors. He is also their international representative and travels widely. He has worked hard himself to get a degree in theology by distance learning from Miami. Fernando is always a step ahead of the others as they come out of their gypsy traditions one by one to have their minds renewed and he loves to discuss his ideas with Desmond. Some years back the women were not allowed to do anything in their services except to lead the singing but never of course from the platform. Fernando has been a pioneer in that area, beginning with his wife, and in the course of time there was a little more freedom for ladies. Fernando's wife has difficulty reading like most of the older gypsy ladies. The men however still sit on one side of the church with the women and children on the other side. The musicians are mostly self-taught but very talented.

Their music is often flamenco and they write many of their own songs and produce many DVDs. Once we had a group of them sing in our church when the Catholic Archbishop was present. In fact he was sitting right behind them and since he is an older man, I was very concerned that the music would be too loud for his ears. I need not have worried. The priest who always accompanies the Archbishop assured me that the loudness was no problem. His words were,

'They are so anointed that their music does us all a lot of good.'

THE CHALLENGE OF JOINT EVENTS. Fernando and some of the gypsies were keen to have more joint events with us. We tried with the *Council of Evangelical Churches* but it did not really work. Fernando and Desmond had an idea when a new congress hall was opened in Badajoz. They decided to organise a joint conference including churches from Portugal. We were the very first group to use the hall the day after its official inauguration. Busloads of people arrived as a child from the Harpenden Christian School had seen in his prayers many years before.

The gypsy children have a reputation for being rather unruly in the meetings. In fact they had no special activities for children until our arrival in Badajoz when they asked for our help in this. We arranged for some gifted children's workers to come over from our church in the UK and also a YWAM team which helped them get started. We also invited the pastor's wife from our Córdoba church, who is particularly gifted with children to help at the joint conference. She and her team had a well-prepared programme for them. What we did not realise was that the parents tried to get their children to go to the meetings. But most of them escaped and they ran around all over the building on the first day. Some even damaged books on the bookstall that the *Christian Literature Crusade* had brought especially from Madrid. There was so much litter in the entrance hall that the cleaners refused to clean it up. Another missionary and I had to do the job.

The second day we were much more strict. The pastors and missionaries sat in the front of the hall and I got tired of all the gypsy pastors' children running in and out.

'Have this sheet of paper' I told them, 'and illustrate the sermon in some way or other. I am offering a prize'.

The pictures they produced were something I treasured for some time. There were obviously budding artists among them. Poor Fernando was so apologetic about the behaviour of his people at that congress, but it did highlight the difficulties in working too closely together.

One positive thing in the conference was that we were able to honour the pastors' wives. We brought them up to the platform on one occasion and some were in tears. They told me afterwards that they were not used to being noticed much though they had to work so hard behind their husbands. The gypsy pastors usually support themselves by selling in the market every morning. Most evenings they have meetings since many of their congregations cannot read. I often found that these ladies look much older than they actually are. It is no doubt because of the hectic lifestyle they have to lead.

GYPSIES IN OUR CHURCH. Over the years we have had some in our church as well. They particularly appreciated the freedom we gave to women and two were part of our leadership team. They had tremendous faith but were not easy to work with because of their strong traditions. I remember taking one gypsy lady, Nina, to a conference in the UK. She had never been in an aeroplane before but was completely at ease. The take-off was delayed because there was some suspicious luggage on board. Eventually the police came and one passenger was taken off the plane and not allowed to travel. Some got in a panic, imagining that something dangerous had been left on board.

One Spanish lady in particular was going to leave. Nina did not hesitate to assure her

'I have prayed and I know we are all going to be safe'.

The lady stayed and Nina spent the rest of the journey testifying to her. In the end however they and we realised that the gypsies were best dealing with their own people. One who had come from the gypsy church had been helping us with the outreach in Corte de Pelea. When he left to return there we arranged that he continue that outreach but under the wing of the gypsy church.

Desmond and I both feel that our lives have been enriched by our contacts and friendships with these lovely people.

25 CHRISTIAN EDUCATION IN SPAIN

HOME-SCHOOLING IN CÓRDOBA. Our son Michael at age four attended quite an elite kindergarten in Córdoba. As a teacher and coming from a family of teachers, education was very important to me. We visited many establishments before deciding on this one. It was modern and the teachers assured us that Michael had fitted in well. However, at home we were seeing something different. From being a happy, contented child, he changed to being extremely restless and we couldn't understand why. Our YWAM friends had already started to talk to us about home-schooling and I began to read all the books and information I could get my hands on. When we finally took him out of the school at age five and began teaching him at home, he said to us,

'This school' (that is mum teaching him in his bedroom) 'is much better than my other one and please don't send me back there'.

Since we were foreigners educating our own son in Spain the authorities did not interfere. We were able to think and pray a lot about what we wanted to teach him. Suddenly we found ourselves re-thinking what we had known of school and education. God became the centre of our school curriculum, not just something tagged on at the end. We, along with another church member, went to a conference on Christian education in Switzerland run by YWAM. Paul Hawkins came to speak from the YWAM university in Hawaii and that opened our eyes even more about the humanistic philosophy behind most educational programmes. He had some statistics from missionary children mentioned in the American edition of *Who's Who*. The conclusion was that these stood out by far from any of the other children of professionals. They were the ones later in places of influence in America. That increased our faith a lot in what we were doing.

HELP WITH THE PROJECT. It was a lonely path to home educate in those days and I was very grateful for the American material given to me by American YWAMers. My sister who was a primary school teacher at that time also provided a lot of help. One year, Susan Chappell, an English assistant in Córdoba who became part of our church, helped us by reading to him on a regular basis. We packed the car with English books and cornflakes, unavailable then in our part of Spain, but still we never had enough. In the end we had to keep them up in a very high cupboard and ration them out from time to time. In all it was a walk of faith and I remember praying *Lord, if he ends up without achieving much, it doesn't matter as long as he follows you!* Not many understood what we were doing and indeed argued with us but we knew God had spoken and that was sufficient for us.

MONTESSORI PRE-SCHOOL. We didn't want to be selfish in giving this special education to our son and forget the church children so we opened a small pre-school in our church building in Córdoba. There we used the Montessori method and the young folk in our church spent hours making lots of materials in wood that would have been impossible for us to buy. The method was so new in Spain that we had several come from other pre-schools to have a look at it and they were impressed. We were very much pioneering in Christian Education in Spain and sad when the school had to be closed down because of our sabbatical year. However, we sowed a seed and it was good on a recent visit to meet a small group from our church in Córdoba now trying to open a Christian school there.

AN OUTSTANDING PROPHECY FULFILLED. There were no home-schooled children in the area but we got to know a Spanish family in Madrid who had six children and all were being taught at home. We became good friends and from time to time we went up to stay with them for a few days. They were also pastors of a church where some of its members lived in community so it was easy for us to find accommodation. We suddenly remembered a specific prophecy we had been given by our good friend Stanley in 1975 in Londonderry.

'You will stay with a man in Madrid who is fat and bald and often wears a blue checked shirt. He has six children and a wife who is very pleasant. One of the children will become sick and you will pray and see them healed.'

Every detail mentioned came true. We took this as confirmation that we were in God's ways. We still have a folder at home where we keep all the prophecies given to us since 1973. Others I have kept in my hand bag at times and they are always a good encouragement to read over from time to time when the going is tough.

The first year we were home-schooling, Paco González, already mentioned in chapter nine, was living with us and watching this phenomenon with great scepticism. He often relates this in conferences and yet God spoke to him even then and he became very influential on a national level in the area of home-schooling. In fact, he has often been on Spanish television talking about the subject and with his two daughters who were home-schooled. He has organised several conferences at which I had the privilege to speak. He was also Headmaster of the Christian school set up by YWAM in Seville. The leader of the base was then the German pastor we had worked with at the beginning of our time in Spain. This pastor always claims our home-schooling had made him too revise his ideas about education.

RESULTS OF HOME-SCHOOLING. When we came to live in Bangor, Northern Ireland in 1984 it was a real test of the education we had given our son. He was just two months away from the dreaded eleven plus examination. In fact, the headmaster was very reluctant to admit him in case he would damage their reputation as a school with excellent eleven plus results. They questioned him being an only child, having lived abroad and being home-schooled; three reasons they claimed that he might not fit into their school. Two months later the headmaster called us in to tell us

'You two have given your son an education fit for a king!'

This was such a surprise after the first difficult meeting we had had with him. Now he was so full of praise for what we had done that I simply burst into tears there in his office. I had had so much self-doubt about this home-schooling. Once again, we saw the blessing of obedience though I had struggled at times. His questions on science and maths had become too much for me. Desmond then decided to give him those lessons at 8.00 am each day. Years later my sister was at a teacher's conference where the lecturer was showing some work done by an 'outstanding pupil' he had had some years before. My sister was thrilled to see the name on the work and realise it was her nephew Michael.

When he went to a grammar school at age eleven, I had the opportunity to teach him French on quite a few occasions. The French teacher was often ill and I was called in at short notice. There I could notice how he was so influenced by the other children and his attention span was a lot worse than when I home-schooled him. In fact, I watched to my dismay his school report go down as well during that year. However, when he moved to the Christian school in England, I had the joy of seeing him very interested again in his studies and after a short while he was moved up a year. That showed me the importance of the learning atmosphere for children.

We had always prayed that he would discover his destiny and not just choose a career that we had wanted for him. Suddenly he arrived home from the Christian school one day, announcing to us,

'I'm going to be a pilot'.

The headmaster had been speaking about Psalm 37:4 'Delight yourself in the Lord and He will give you the desires of your heart.' He encouraged the pupils to pray about the dreams and desires God had put in their hearts and believe they would be fulfilled. We were shocked as it was not the easiest time economically in our lives. We had just moved over to England and were paying a large mortgage. *Could we ever afford it and was he really good enough to become a pilot?* All my doubts surfaced again about the education I had given him. Fortunately, we didn't share our doubts with him and left it at that. Over the years we have learnt that the enemy will attack us with doubts when we try to obey God's plans for our lives. We will always be indebted to the headmaster and staff of that school for putting such an emphasis on character training and destiny as well as the academic side.

CAPTAIN BELLEW

Before going to university, he applied to British Airways only to be told that they were not taking in any new pilots. Instead, he went on to study aeronautical engineering. After graduating with an MSc he worked for the Ministry of Defence for a year before applying again. This time he got an interview lasting two days. He rang during that period to say he had never prayed so much in this life as the essay he was given to write was impossible! There were 47,000 applicants and only 120 were chosen. Out of that number 13 were selected to do their training in Australia and he was one of them. The week before, he had also had a four-day interview with the Royal Air Force. There he had got down to the last round and they offered him a place as a navigator, saying that with time he would train as a pilot. As a mother, I was quite relieved when he chose the BA offer. Otherwise he could have found himself in the Iraq war and dealing with post-traumatic stress as many RAF pilots have, after coping with bombing and loss of life. Once again we had seen God's faithfulness to us as a family. The Bible shows us 'He is no man's debtor.'

We have since enjoyed of course the blessing of obedience with Michael's education as he has found his destiny as a pilot with British Airways. While still training in Australia, he was able to take my sister and me on a flight in a very small plane. It was thrilling to hear him say

'Mum, I know God has made me for this. I just love flying'.

He now is one of the top 10% in BA as a training captain and gives regular courses to other pilots.

When we had our first flight with him, as his Christmas present to us, we remembered a prophecy he had been given at his baptism.

'You will be a leader of men and indeed companies of men. You will travel the world but not in the missionary sense of the word like your parents' were some of the exact words.

We didn't understand it at the time but now we remember it each time we enjoy a flight with him and realise how so many lives are in his hands. Moreover, he can pass or fail many pilots and captains in the company. He has, like his parents, found his destiny.

Once he was a pilot, I had lots of congratulations, even from those who had questioned us about home-schooling and sending him to a Christian school. I was interviewed or asked to write articles on several occasions in Spain where home-schooling is still very much a grey area. There were opportunities to talk to folk who were influential in the teaching profession and teachers' unions. It is neither legal nor illegal so is discussed a lot. Fourteen families at the last count have been taken to court because they had taken their children out of the system to home-school them. All eventually won their cases. I sometimes had the job of encouraging these families or at least praying for them. On one internet news programme where I was interviewed, they were particularly interested in the results of this kind of education. I expressed my views on education as a Christian and how that had encouraged me to home-school. Unfortunately that part did not appear on the programme. Only the fact that a British child home-schooled in Spain was now a pilot with British Airways, that well-known and greatly admired airline.

CHRISTIAN SCHOOLS IN SPAIN. When investigating for my book on Christian Education I was able to visit some of the Christian schools in Spain. The best known ones are those begun by the Fliedner family. El Porvenir and Juan de Valdés are large schools still in Madrid. They were two of the first schools to take in the wave of South American immigrants, a big challenge in itself. They even attended to the material needs of the families of the children they were educating. Federico Fliedner was that famous German missionary who worked in Spain from 1869-1901. He was a pastor, an educator, a writer, a poet, a New Testament translator, an editor and a philanthropist. He believed that every church should have its own school. I had the honour of visiting his granddaughter Doña Elfriede just before she died. She expressed to me,

'How difficult it has been working with Christian schools in Spain. My family has had had many obstacles to overcome.'

In 1932 there were 171 school teachers teaching 7,459 pupils in Christian schools throughout Spain. However, many of these schools were closed down during the civil war, or later, by Franco.

Doña Elfreide came alive when she started to share with me how some of their past pupils were now impacting the evangelical world and Spanish society in general.

Another school I visited was the Alpha and Omega school in Denia, Alicante. This has been a venture of faith by Jorge Pastor, now a retired Baptist pastor and ex-President of the Baptist Union in Spain. When I visited, I discovered that 98% of the pupils at that time come from Catholic families, reflecting the good reputation it had in the area. A publishing company was so impressed by what they saw in the primary end of the school that they asked the teachers to write a textbook. I was very impressed with the family atmosphere in the school. There are a few other smaller Christian schools in the country and I am glad to say that my book has had a small influence. I am still in contact with groups in Madrid, Seville, Badajoz and Córdoba who are in the process of setting up schools despite the many battles they have had and are still having.

RELIGIOUS EDUCATION IN STATE SCHOOLS. It was only in 1992 that Protestants were given the right to give Religious Education classes in state schools. This was a result of the Law of Religious liberty in 1980 and the agreements later signed by the Federation of Religious Establishments with the State. We were delighted when one of our members in Badajoz, Sonia Algado, a primary schoolteacher, recently finished the intensive training course. Sonia is the first Protestant to be teaching R.E. in four different schools in the city.

OTHER ACTIVITIES IN CHRISTIAN EDUCATION. In 2006 I published a book on the subject for the Spanish speaking world as there was little if anything written on it then. I called it *Aventuras De Fe... La Educación Cristiana* (In English *Adventures Of Faith...Christian Education*) and soon sold 500 copies. I had been encouraged to write by several people, including Gabino Fernández, the outstanding historian and ex-pastor. He wrote a chapter for me on the history of Christian Education in Spain. Without his advice I don't think I would have taken on such a daunting task. The publishing company later wanted me to produce a revised edition but I simply didn't have

Aventuras de Fe...

La Educación Cristiana

CAROLINA BELLEW

Con la colaboración de Gabino Fernández Campos

time. There was too much to be done in the churches that we were establishing.

I was an avid member of the *Association of Evangelical Educators* that met in Madrid and though it was a considerable distance to travel, I was grateful to folk such as Dr Raúl García (a children's psychiatrist from there) and David and Priscilla Pritchard. They were British missionaries and representatives for *Scripture Union* and *Godly play* material in Spain. They usually put me up and on one occasion suggested a one day conference for me. That was especially for training of Christian teachers of English who came from all parts of the country. As a result, I became a friend and advisor for some of them. I also twice had the honour of representing this association in a European conference on Christian Education called *EurECA*. That was in 2001 and again in 2009. This brought together Christian educators both from Christian and state schools, some holding influential positions in their different countries. In February 2009 I had the privilege of taking a Spanish lady to the Christian Schools Trust conference in England. This brought back memories of the very first conference I had attended for Christian schools many years before in Southampton, England. On that occasion I was taken by a group of Spanish and Argentine teachers from a small school in Madrid which later closed.

CHRISTIAN SCHOOLS IN SOUTH AMERICA. Christian schools in South America on the other hand are popular as I discovered when investigating for my book. When on a ministry trip to Patagonia, Argentina, Pastor Daniel Chamorro organised for us to stay with an outstanding lady, Betty Mancini. Betty not only was an Inspector of Education in the state system responsible for 49 schools, but also a headmistress of a large school in her husband's church. He was a prominent renewed Baptist pastor who earned his living as a dentist in Buenos Aires. She took us to visit about six different Christian schools in the same city. I was able to interview the headmasters in each school. Some claimed to be so successful that they accounted for some of the tremendous growth in the churches there. The oldest one belonged to the Methodist church and has a beautiful building and spacious grounds in the elite area of Buenos Aires. It now serves the wealthy and influential families of the city because of its excellent education.

In Patagonia I visited several large Christian schools as well in March 2001. The one in Plottier in Pastor Daniel Chamorro's church was impressive. Daniel runs an apostolic network of churches in Argentina, Spain, Italy and India. This visit was significant as later we decided to leave our Spanish churches officially under his care when we returned to the UK in 2013. His church and school building was burnt down, probably by drug lords as so many drug addicts had been converted through his ministry. When we arrived, the church members, though still shocked, had just finished re-constructing their building at great personal expense. The teachers had even decorated the classrooms themselves in most artistic ways.

There are some English-speaking Christian schools in Spain. One recently opened in Fuengirola belongs to the well-known church 'The Ark' and has a long waiting list I believe. This is normal in whatever country these Christian schools are found. When we return to God's plan for education with Him in the centre instead of man-centred education, good results will follow.

26 OUR LAST YEARS IN SPAIN

A VISIT TO A CHURCH PLANT IN POLAND. In 2009 we were invited to minister in a church plant in Poland. This was a very enjoyable trip and the Polish pastor and we had much to share with one another. We were both living in very Catholic countries where progress is slow for evangelical churches.

The last four years we spent in Badajoz were some of the most fruitful and happy years of our life. We realised we were getting older and needed to think of a successor for the work. A Spanish couple had considered coming to our town but in the end, went elsewhere. We later realised that God had protected our church for soon their marriage broke up. *Who will continue to pastor this church?* we often asked ourselves.

A lovely young couple came from the UK and it was felt that they were the couple to follow on from us. After several years pastoring the church, while we sought to open a new church in La Roca de la Sierra, they decided it was not for them. They had a vision for a 'café church or simple church' and wanted to start that in Badajoz with some of our folk. We found ourselves having to take up the church pastorate again while we thought we were preparing to move back to the UK. Although we prayed for them and gave them gifts in recognition of their service to the church, we were sad to see them go. A number of our people went with them, including most of our leadership team. Sadly, with the passage of time this vision did not prosper and eventually their church was discontinued. Attempts have been made before in larger cities in Spain to have alternative types of church but not with much success. It is different in the UK or the USA.

When the dust settled, the church had been reduced to less than half its original size, so it took some time to build it up again. We had to form a new leadership team and find some new leaders for the cell groups etc. We were very grateful to Raul and Elisabet Villamil (Columbian missionaries with six children). This family travelled each week to help us in the church for six months before planting their own church in Mérida.

The Catholic Archbishop had suggested we do a trial run of an Alpha Course with four priests and four Protestant pastors, before running it in all the Catholic parishes in Extremadura. We were unable to find time to do this with all the unexpected changes. We had to leave Spain without seeing that happen. This made us sad that we had missed such an opportunity.

We soon saw rapid growth and a strong presence of God in our meetings. Within two years the church had recovered numerically and went on to surpass its previous size, becoming one of the largest non-gypsy churches in Extremadura. What particularly delighted us was to see more and more Spaniards come into our meetings. We had a very multi-cultural church like the church at Antioch. It was such a joy to see Spaniards and Latin Americans mixing well. As the Latin Americans matured they learnt how to humbly receive the Spaniards into the church. We had so many baptisms during the winter that we decided to build a baptismal tank under the platform of our building. Baptisms in the open air were fine in summer but in winter, even in Spain, it is too cold for that.

Once after attending a very powerful conference in the USA I had dreams almost every night for a month. While some of the dreams were warnings about things that would later happen, others brought back fearful scenes from my youth. Each morning we were able to pray over these and I believe God healed those memories. I particularly appreciated Joyce Meyer's teaching on the emotions and renewing of the mind.

'Worry is pride,' she says, 'since we don't trust God we try a back-up plan in case God doesn't come through. It is OK to ponder and pray but not get into anxiety.'

In Badajoz we enjoyed the benefits of the Spanish Health Service which proved to be very good. Desmond had two experiences with hospitals. The first was when our church building was flooded. Waters came up from the sewers and with that all the rat infections etc. He ended up doing most of the cleaning up and soon had to go into hospital with pneumonia. They asked him,

'Have you been working with animals as the tests have shown that up?'

The second was when he had a sudden heart attack in January 2013 just three months before we returned to live in the UK. Again, the care was excellent. Badajoz is not a tourist area so they are not so used to English patients. This was probably to our advantage as the hospital staff pulled out all the stops to make sure we were well treated.

Within a few hours I was inundated with mobile phone messages from church members and all the pastors of the town, offering any help that was needed. A Catholic priest also offered to be put on the list to drive me to the hospital. With such love and care all around me it was as if I was being carried along in the Father's arms despite the stressful situation. I once heard a famous preacher say that if we feel and sense a lot of God's love for us, we can overcome anything.

NEW GROWTH AMONG THE SPANIARDS. One story will serve to illustrate this new growth. Imagine a skinny, wizened and worn 50 year old lady. Her daughter was in a church in Cáceres and one day was in tears with me about her family. Both her parents had been on drugs for years and her brothers seemed to be in and out of prison. Desmond went to visit one of her brothers, Pedro, who that very evening repented and came back to God. He had been, we discovered, at one time, part of a gypsy church. That evening his mother, Felisa, also made a profession of faith in Christ and promised to come to church the following Sunday. I was shocked at her physical appearance when I met her. A life of drug addiction had taken its toll. Felisa, as a Spaniard, was very touched by the love shown to her by the Latin Americans in the church. Before long she was firmly established in her new-found faith. For weeks we enjoyed her testimonies as each Sunday she wanted to share her battles and victories with drugs and cigarettes.

Soon her common law husband noticed the great difference, although she had separated from him by then, and he too came and accepted God as his Saviour. Brothers followed and a sister with two very unruly children. An uncle came who was an alcoholic and drug abuser as well as a bingo addict and had lost his wife because of it. His mentally retarded daughter came too and hugged everybody each meeting as she sensed the love there was in the church. He believed in Jesus the first time he came to the church and months passed before he could get through a service without being in tears. Another relative came who was a witch and he remarked to Desmond afterwards about the 'energy' that was coming from us both. Unfortunately, he never came back. We did have folk that had been very involved in the occult and it was quite a long battle sometimes to see them completely free.

Felisa's appearance changed dramatically as God began to work in her life. She found a job cleaning the home of a lady who owned a boutique. She gave her lots of clothes so Felisa arrived in church looking even more attractive. Before long one of the older men from Uruguay, took a great interest in her so we had to talk to her. She suddenly disclosed the fact

'I have never been actually married to the man you think is my husband. Yes, he is the father of my five grown up children but he has treated me so badly, especially when on drugs. I refuse to go back to him!'

This man had noticed the interest from the Uruguayan and was not having it. In fact, he attacked him one day with a hatchet outside his flat and the police were called in. It was going to be complicated to have these two men in our church and we were quite relieved when the ex-partner went off to the Pentecostal church in the town. Felisa never married the Uruguayan as she didn't think he was a keen enough Christian but I am glad to be able to say that she and her ex-partner were eventually married and are still following the Lord. Violence was often very common among these fiery Latin Americans. I didn't preach a lot in the church but I remember having to prepare a message on domestic violence which was a relevant topic for many in our congregation.

A WEDDING WITH A DIFFERENCE. Another interesting Colombian couple joined us. They had just got out of prison for drug smuggling. As a result of a grandmother's prayers in Colombia, Elisabet had come to her senses when in Badajoz prison and returned to the God she had known as a child. She looked for a church and brought along her partner in crime. Omar soon repented and became a Christian. After we baptised them, they asked us to marry them. It was a wedding with a difference.

They did not want anyone to know about the wedding in case they would bring presents. We announced it as a surprise event for the church so folks turned up and were surprised to see a marriage ceremony. The bride was dressed in a simple white trouser suit and the groom also in white clothes that were not new. Elisabet and Omar said they had spent so many years carried away by consumerism and trying to become rich and everything had gone wrong for them. They therefore wanted to have the simplest wedding possible. They testified to the landlord of the apartment they were renting and he and his wife (a retired Spanish couple from Barcelona) also became part of our church in La Roca de la Sierra.

WORSHIP. Worship was an interesting area in our churches. Many wanted to sing and be involved in the worship but their musical skills were sadly lacking. We were grateful to foreigners who came to give music courses now and again. This branch of the church always gave me a lot of pain. However, God must have a sense of humour. My husband and I were suddenly chosen with three other pastors to be on the advisory board for the *Marcos Witt School of Music*. Marcos Witt is one of the most famous musicians and song writers in the Latin American world with his schools of music well established there in many countries. He opened his first music school in Valencia and they would have liked us to somehow open one in Extremadura but it never happened. We had enough just getting worship going in our churches.

Tamara from Slovakia who was working with her husband in Extremadura with the mission *World Vision* gave voluntary singing lessons to many in our congregations. Luz Denia's two children, now teenagers and accomplished musicians gave keyboard and guitar lessons to others. Those who couldn't sing in tune worked hard and improved. In fact, one Colombian lady Clarissa told me.

'I have a vision to make a CD with me and my daughter singing the many songs I have written'.

I confess to being a little sceptical about how she would ever do it but fortunately I kept silent. Clarissa was able to see her vision fulfilled, making two CDs and now sells many of these to help fund our mission work in India. It was a lesson to me once more that God doesn't always look on the natural ability but He looks on the heart.

HISTORY MAKERS. We were blessed with the arrival of *History Makers* twice in our area. This is an international movement that looks for young leaders who they hope will make history in their churches and nations. Nino Riquelme and his wife Paty brought it to our attention since we had become firm friends. This is a couple of church-planters from YWAM Chile who came to live and plant a church in Merida during our last years in Spain. Nine of our young people enrolled for this very intensive week-long course which the church partially paid for. Desmond was invited as one of the speakers and a second shorter course was then held in our church. Each time the young people came back on fire for God and went out on the streets to evangelise.

As a result of the impact of History Makers one eighteen-year-old Bolivian called Richard decided to go to Cáceres to do a discipleship training school with YWAM. This was very significant as the church regarded him as their very own missionary and rose to the financial challenge. Many promised finance for him. YWAM felt that was a great example for the churches of the region who all complained they could not support a student for the school.

LA ROCA CHURCH PLANT. La Roca de la Sierra church progressed and we decided to rent premises and formally become a church. This was a great occasion and many other pastors from Extremadura came to support us on that special day in 2010. Oscar and his wife had pioneered the work along with us and are now pioneering another church plant. Enrique and Luz Denia then became the pastors of the work and suddenly they told us they believed they should actually go and live in the village.

'Are you absolutely sure about this decision?' we asked them both.

INAUGURATION.(From left to right) CATHOLIC PRIEST,
PRESIDENT EVANGELICAL COUNCIL OF EXTREMADURA,
MAYOR, DESMOND AND PASTOR ENRIQUE

COUPLES' DINNER AND MARRIAGE TALK

This represented a very big sacrifice as they both had to leave their jobs in Badajoz. They were also leaving their nice flat that they were buying and had to rent a much poorer one. The eldest daughter doing A-Level's was to live in the flat on her own to finish off her education. Their two younger children had to change schools and the village education is usually a little behind the schools in the city.

However, as we all prayed about it we saw that it was right for them. We warned them well of the difficulties they might experience. In fact, it was very difficult for them both with employment and the church. Quite a lot of people have been converted, including friends of their children but not so many have stayed the course. In a village the neighbours talk a lot together and anyone who dares to leave the traditional church can be ostracised.

They have done a lot to break those barriers down, especially by helping poorer Spaniards with food and clothing. In fact one TV channel came to do a programme on the village and they were urged by neighbours to interview Enrique. Although he constantly tried his best to stop them, many in the village continued to call him 'Father Enrique'. They filmed him taking food to a needy family and asked him to do a mock service there and then which was televised. Enrique was somewhat of a novelty for them: here was a man from a poor country himself helping the poor in prosperous Spain. Two political parties have tried to persuade him to stand as mayor but he declined. He did not want to be diverted from his main purpose of church work.

His family have got on well too despite all our doubts. Victor, their nineteen-year-old son did a DTS course with YWAM and was on their staff for a few years. His parents found it impossible to fund this long-expressed desire to join that mission. Somehow or other the Brazilian director of the nearby base, recognising his musical gifts and his unique situation, found a grant for him. That at the time was quite unusual in YWAM circles.

NEW ARRIVALS. In Badajoz we benefited from the arrival of a young Brazilian lady called Juliana. She had been an airhostess

ENRIQUE, LUZ DENIA & FAMILY

with Qatar Airways and had suffered a lot there for her faith. She had the typical Brazilian enthusiasm for the work of God and brought in folk from the street quite regularly. Not all, I must add, were genuine seekers. She was so attractive but also naive, not realising that many men were really only interested in her rather than in God. I had to save her on a few occasions from unwanted male attention. She began a group for the over eighteen young people. Unfortunately, she did not manage to renew her papers and had to go back to her own country.

We were blessed by Gloria and José Carlos, another Colombian couple who arrived in our last years. They were relatives of others already established in the church. They were well-trained in different areas of ministry and leadership in a church that was part of the G12 movement in their own country. This is a global cell-church discipleship movement. We had received other potential leaders from Venezuela, Costa Rica and Brazil who turned out to be problematic, but these two were different. They came with such a servant heart and never tried to impose on us the vision from their own very successful church. They had a lovely family and told us

'Our strength is in giving marriage courses.'

The courses normally finished with a special 'Renewal of vows' ceremony. In some miraculous way the ladies usually managed to get beautiful second-hand wedding dresses for the occasion. There were lots of tears and emotion.

Only Desmond and I knew the amazing stories of grace behind many of the couples, the number of times we had been called to the homes of some of them because they were about to separate. Many had not had a church wedding. As they allowed God to deal with them, it was such a pleasure to see their love for their spouse blossom and increase. We saw once more that our God unites rather than divides.

Gloria was extremely sensitive in the spiritual world. Once towards the end of our time in Spain, when I was worried about our house, her husband told me how she had seen an archangel guarding it, as she came to our gate. That was needless to say an encouragement to us both, especially as we were already home in the UK three years before it sold.

We were often amazed at the sensitivity of the Latin Americans. A Brazilian pastor and his wife came to the church for about a year. He had had some bad experiences in Spain and they were grateful for the time of healing and refreshment they experienced with us. The husband brought some impressive Brazilian pastors to our church. One told me that I had had a visit from an angel without realising it and he quoted the exact day and hour from the previous week. In fact, that very day I was so aware of God's presence in our lounge that I had not been able to move much all afternoon and had related the incident to Desmond. This pastor organised several visits to churches in Portugal where Desmond preached. We also represented the churches in Extremadura at a large conference in Alentejo (the neighbouring region to us in Portugal). It brought back to our minds that vision Desmond had had when in Córdoba that we would move to work in Extremadura and even into Portugal.

We had other so-called pastors, from Brazil in particular, who managed to deceive us into giving money to pay their debts. Promises were often made of re-payment but few actually did. You need so much discernment in this day and age. Another Brazilian couple were a real blessing to the church. They were recently married. The wife, Mona Lisa, daughter of a pastor in the Church of the Nazarene, had to come to Badajoz for a year as part of her PhD research in water purification. The husband was a musician. Since he was not allowed to work in Spain he gave his services to our church and indeed also to the wider church. He set up a simple recording studio in his flat and was able to make the first CD for our church with several singers and musicians taking part.

BECOMING 'PARENTS' AT A NEARBY YWAM BASE. Suddenly we received a phone call from Alfonso Cherene, one of the YWAM leaders. He is a Brazilian who has spent many years with the mission in Spain.

'I am bringing a young Brazilian down to visit you who believes he has a call to set up a base in Extremadura,' he told us in a very excited voice.

Junior arrived in our home and we connected at once. We were able to introduce him at the Evangelical Council leaders' meeting. When the base was finally set up in Cáceres, we became the official 'parents' of the base. The national leaders in Madrid wanted to be sure that these very zealous young Brazilians would have someone with experience in the area. This was to guide them in their early years in Spanish society.

Once again as in Córdoba many years before, we began to have YWAM groups to help out in our churches particularly with the youth work. It was a joy to be able to go off on a journey, knowing that we had left the church in capable hands. At times a team of ten or more would stay in our home and we always returned to find everything immaculate. Before we left Spain, we were amazed to enjoy a moving farewell ceremony at their Cáceres base. They even gave us a donation, which is typical of the faith and generosity we have experienced with this mission.

A NEW INTERCESSORS GROUP. During the last few years I began to understand the need for personal intercessors for Desmond and myself. Now we are very grateful for all the folk from our home churches and beyond who faithfully prayed for us over the years. A Latin American lady came through our church who told me how she and two other ladies had faithfully interceded for her pastor and his wife in Colombia. The Hebrew word for intercession means 'touching' or 'connecting'. I began to understand that the intercessor is plugging the gaps where the enemy can get in.

After reading an up-to-date book on intercession I began with Maruja, Berta, Oscar's mother, and Lupe, a mature lady from Ecuador. I shared our personal burdens with these three dear ladies, knowing that nothing would be divulged to the rest of our churches. Maruja had been well prepared for this task by her sister Piedy, a very experienced intercessor living in Basingstoke. We were amazed at the number of answers to prayer we saw in those years both personally and in the churches.

NEW INITIATIVES. We enjoyed other initiatives from the church members. One lady began a very successful church newsletter complete with photos, interviews, reflections, news and poems. The art work was impressive too. Another soldier who was specialised in First Aid gave a ten week course on that. I benefited from that as well as the many carers we had in the church looking after the elderly with very little preparation for the task.

Another highlight was an hour long live interview with Revelation TV who have their studio in La Cala, near Málaga. They were particularly interested in hearing about our work.

NEW PASTORS FOR OUR MAIN CHURCH PLANT. The years were going by and we still had no pastor to take our place. Our three grandchildren were rapidly growing up and we were missing those early years of their childhood. We began to receive emails from the British organisation called *Christian Concern* and we realised that the UK also needed a Christian voice. Daniel Chamorro from Argentina whom we had known for many years, suggested to us,

'My nephew Christian, and Raquel his Spanish wife, might be suitable pastors to succeed you.'

We prayed about it and it seemed right. The church also agreed to it. In September 2012 they were set in as pastors. We had finally managed to sell our English Academy so could move forward towards our return to the UK.

FAREWELLS AND RETURN TO UK. We finally got here on 10 April 2013 after several moving farewell ceremonies. The first was at the annual gathering of the churches in Plasencia (the nearest event in Extremadura to the UK *Big Church Day Out*). Desmond was the guest speaker at what became our farewell service with all the churches in Extremadura.

Then some of the churches invited us specially to speak at their Sunday service and gave us a farewell. The Brazilian Presbyterian Church in Don Benito was a memorable occasion. About 200 people arrived at our last farewell in Badajoz. It was a lovely surprise to see many of our neighbours in our church for the first time. Twelve came from my Portuguese class though I had left that

OUR ENGLISH ACADEMY PUBLICITY

a year before. All the pastors from Badajoz and some from beyond came forward to pray for us. These included our Catholic priest friend who has a lot of responsibility in the diocese. He shared some words of appreciation and presented us with a large Catholic Bible. Other presents were given which we treasure today and display in our lounge. Iain & Pat Anderson from *Southampton Community Church* also spoke. They had often visited and advised us through the years.

We were back three years in the UK before managing to sell our house in Spain. We had to accept a very reduced price, only half of the house price we are now in. If we had come home some years before the property market crashed in Spain, as we wanted to but were unable to find a successor, we would have been much better off. However, we were reminded once more that following God abroad can be costly: no pain, no gain!

The handover period was easy as Christian and Raquel were so full of respect for us and what we had built up. We too respected their different method of handling the church so we have an excellent relationship. Each time we return to Badajoz we are warmly welcomed both by them and the congregation of course as well. It is a joy to see the church still growing from strength to strength.

I came back to the UK a very different person from when I first went to Spain. God had done a deep work in my life changing so many of my fears to faith. In the last years we had a few court cases where we were accused unjustly. One of these even dragged on for two years after we left Spain. As our lawyer pointed out, some Spaniards believe we foreigners have lots of money and will try anything to get some from us. Glad to say we won the cases and I was amazed at the peace I had throughout the whole process.

It has been a big change for us settling back into life in the UK. At first, we felt very like foreigners in our own country but with time it becomes easier. God has opened up new areas of service both in a local church and representing our church in a *Churches Together* committee to organise joint events. We are working on a follow-up booklet *Reflections on Missionary Strategy for Spain*. We are also involved with Latin American fellowships and churches in the area, as well as making ministry trips to Spain and Brazil. It is a new season for us but also the beginning of another adventure of faith. As someone once said

'The whole of life is an adventure and we have to squeeze the last drop out of it'.

When we meet up with friends old and new we may not be able to share about our latest cruise holiday but we are grateful for energy and health compared to many folk our age. We can share about the colourful characters that came into our churches and into our lives. This book has only touched on some of them. Life in the land of the matador has been a great adventure, very fulfilling and a life-changing experience. SOLI DEO GLORIA.

WHAT NOW?

If you have any further questions or concerns, please don't hesitate to contact us at the following email addresses.
carolinabellew@gmail.com
ramonbellew@gmail.com

You may want to PRAY. We can send you topics for prayer as we regularly visit our churches and other churches in Spain where we have relationships.

You may want to GO. We ourselves go sometimes taking teams with us so you could join us. We can put you in touch with people, missions and churches all over the nation.

You may want to GIVE through our charity to the many church planters we have left behind. These are often Latin Americans who have VERY FEW resources. Some have become Christians in Spain and have no links with churches in their home countries.

Our charity is FIRST FRUITS Ltd, Charity Number 1125700. All proceeds from the sale of this book will go to FIRST FRUITS and not to us personally.

Caroline Bellew. BA Dip Ed

Caroline has been a foreign language teacher for more than 50 years. She was the founder member of a workgroup for Christian modern language teachers in the UK and co-editor of a magazine called *Language in God's World*. She has lectured at conferences on Christian education both in the UK and Spain. Her first book published in 2006 was in Spanish - *Aventuras de Fe...La Educación Cristiana* (*Adventures of Faith...Christian Education*). With her husband Desmond, she has been leading churches in the UK and Spain, since she was 25 years of age. After 30 years as pioneer evangelists in Spain, planting several churches, they are now part of Arun Community Church in W. Sussex where they live. The church has asked them to lead an evangelism project among the many Portuguese living in the area. They are involved in a nearby Spanish speaking fellowship and help from time to time in a Brazilian church in Hove.

They have been married for 49 years and have one son, Michael. He is married to Kathryn and they have three wonderful children.

Printed in Poland
by Amazon Fulfillment
Poland Sp. z o.o., Wrocław